20/18

AR IPSHITA,
HOPE YOU ENJOY!
LABOR OF LOVE!
SEE YOU AT OTE 7!

SEE YOU

at the

7

STORIES FROM THE
Bay Area's
LAST ORIGINAL
MILE HOUSE

BY VANESSA GARCIA *with* REGINA ABUYUAN

EDITOR
Regina ABUYUAN

BOOK DESIGN
Noel AVENDAÑO

ILLUSTRATIONS
Josh ARGOSINO

_____

Printed in the Philippines.

First printing, 2018

7 Mile House
2800 Bayshore Boulevard
Brisbane, California 94005
U.S.A

www.7milehouse.com

ISBN
978-0-692-99064-3

To my parents, Ogie and Cleo,
who taught me how to uphold my integrity,
that nothing is impossible,
and every problem has a solution.

To my children, Visa and Tylaw,
for their unconditional love as I built the business,
through the late, absent nights so many years ago.
They are a constant reminder to see the goodness
in every soul; my twin heavens on earth.

And to Ambette, who pulls me back to reality
when my head gets stuck in the clouds – but
who lets me fly anyway, because he knows
I'll always come floating back down.

Thank you for always giving me a soft landing.

Table of CONTENTS

F o r e **WORD**

By **CARL NOLTE**

verybody knows about the Golden Gate bridge and the cable cars, but one of the great things about living in the San Francisco Bay Area is that there is a surprise around every corner. One of them the 7 Mile House on Bayshore Boulevard, just outside San Francisco and just inside Brisbane.

One of the biggest surprises is that more people don't know about the 7 Mile House, considering that the place has been there in various forms for one hundred and sixty years. It has a long and colorful past, and a terrific present. History is on the menu at the 7 Mile—along with good drinks, good times, and good music. It's a real find.

I found the 7 Mile House myself only recently, when Ken Sproul, a friend of mine who collects information about interesting restaurants, offered to buy me lunch there. "You'll like it," he said, "This place has a great story."

It starts with the restaurant's unusual name. It was one of a series of "mile houses," which were eating and drinking places set up every mile or so on the road between the San Francisco City Hall and points south. So the 7 Mile House was seven miles from the heart of the city. A journey of that length on horseback, or in a wagon down a dirt road, dusty in the summer and muddy in the winter, was no picnic. After seven miles, most travelers needed a break, maybe a meal, maybe a drink, or maybe….

The first 7 Mile House began life as a simple toll house, where travelers paid a small toll to use the road. It opened for business in 1858, so they say. In those days, California was far away from the rest of the United States, and it wasn't until two years after the 7 Mile House opened that the famous Pony Express began. That means the 7 Mile is one of the oldest eating and drinking places in the United States.

Vanessa Garcia, the owner, manager, and leading light of the 7, tells the tale of her restaurant in this book. This was never one of those fancy-dan places from the Gilded Age. The 7 Mile House has always served the people who built this marvelous region—factory people, railroad men and women, workers who kept the electric wires humming, neighbors from up the road. Ordinary

people, the salt of the earth.

The place had a bit of a shady past at times, usually when the long arm of the law did not extend very far south of the San Francisco County line, especially in a place located in the heart of a place that Vanessa Garcia calls "the middle of nowhere." An old pal remembers meeting a friend in the back room of the place that sounded very familiar. The man had a pile of twenty dollar bills. "See?" he said, "crime does pay."

But that was long ago. The 7 Mile House is a family restaurant now, friendly and charming. It is also a California story from its birth as a wild west roadhouse to its present style as a place with a Filipino-American flavor. Its hamburgers have won awards, too, and even dogs like the 7 Mile; recently, the place won an award as the best dog-friendly restaurant in the region.

You can stop by the 7 Mile House for a good meal and a good time. And you can check out this book for a good tale.

CARL NOLTE
November 2017
San Francisco, California

INTRODUCTION

By **REGINA ABUYUAN**

The author and editor, 1982.

epending on what your prevailing values are, it's easy to take old things for granted. Old houses are left to crumble, old brands renamed and repackaged, old people set conveniently in a corner or retirement home, unmissed and eventually, forgotten.

In the Philippines, where Vanessa and I are from, it is an uphill battle preserving heritage sites and customs. Zoning laws are mostly absent throughout the country, and corruption is rife; every day, millions of pesos exchange hands to get permits to put up commercial cookie-cutter structures side by side ancestral homes that have seen better days. Amongst a people suffering from a collective shortening of memory, we allow sleek new monoliths to take the place of grand old hotels and apartment buildings that were once the toast of Southeast Asia, leave our iconic landmarks to waste away and be taken over by wild vine and vagabonds, and watch as powerful reminders of our past are taken over by new powers that would rather rub out memories than enhance them.

The eradication of physical, brick-and-mortar sites has an effect on the psyche. As the places built during the highest periods of our history as Filipinos disappear, so do pieces of ourselves that should make us truly proud: Our reverence for deep learning and big ideas; our independence of thought, never having to look towards the West for approval; our authentic respect and appreciation towards indigenous art and tradition.

While all things are impermanent and must change with the times, there is unquantifiable value in keeping portions of the past intact—if not through literal preservation, then through documentation. People need a physical place or reminder to fill that space within them that answers to faith, nostalgia, and other abstract human yearnings.

For some, that place can be a church, an old home, a school. A bar.

Vanessa's obsession with the history of 7 Mile House started shortly after she purchased it in 2004, upon learning of its age, and hearing the stories of its previous owner, bookie Al Flynn, and his mother Camille Stuehler, who managed it for fifty years. Notions of producing a book emerged around 2005, and nagged at her every so often. Finally, time and resources aligned in early 2017, and production on *See You at the 7* started in earnest.

When Vanessa first contacted me to help her with this book, we never expected it to become this comprehensive. Our original idea was a collection of little stories and anecdotes, handed down through the years by old regulars and employees of 7 Mile House. These were to be first published as a blog on the restaurant's website. In print form, they would accompany corresponding portraits, with old photos of the bar scattered in between. The concept morphed into something more daunting when she handed me a list of what I was to look for on our first trip to the San Mateo Public Library.

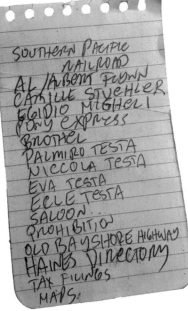

The ease and confidence with which I expected to write this book dissipated. This book had the potential to be more than a compendium of blog posts and as-told-to's. It could be fleshed out with more historical context, more probing into the figures who started it before Lenny and Camille Stuehler—and later, I thought, more questions about how the damned mile houses started, beyond the usual answers about them being pit stops that marked distances from the San Francisco Ferry Building (which we found later was a fallacy). But to achieve this, we would need to do more than interviews. We needed to explore maps and archives; Vanessa even insisted digging up old records at the County Assessor's Office in San Mateo, CalTrans, and going to San Francisco Municipal Transportation Agency. She was right. These offices gave us much vital information and never-before-seen photographs.

The irony of this endeavor was that she had me, an outsider, to help her. Sure, the element of trust was there—we are cousins, after all, second degree cousins who grew up as close as sisters; we know each other's secrets, can predict what the other is going to say. (Workwise, this was an advantage: We completed everything—research, writing, editing, and layouts—in seven months, sans editorial assistant.) But the words on the list Vanessa gave me that day were just that: words, scattered names and places that had no context or meaning. I was even surprised that, given the longevity of 7 Mile House, no one before Vanessa had thought to piece its history together.

Perhaps it had to take Vanessa Garcia, an immigrant from the Philippines, a stubborn, dogged woman who had to work double-, triple-hard to make things work in the United States, to make this book happen. The timing is uncanny, as well: While world leaders promote disunity, suspicion of the outsider and wariness of the different, stories of places like 7 Mile House—a place where ideas that divide us do not exist—should be encouraged and told. It's a story of individuals seizing opportunity no matter how farfetched it seems, of innovation and imagination, of creating a home away from home for all who care to visit, and (hopefully) never having to turn anyone away.

7 Mile House—the stories about it and made within it, as much as the physical place—is an experience that perpetuates itself. It'll be around as long as there's a reason to say, "See you at the 7."

We hope you enjoy our efforts, and that you also learn something new from this book. If not, well then, drop by the restaurant. If the words and photos here don't make you happy, then maybe a San Miguel and *sisig* will.

REGINA ABUYUAN
December 2017
San Felipe, Zambales, Philippines

TIMELINE *of* OWNERSHIP

1858 - 1889
7 Mile House was a toll gate

1889 - 1902
(San Bruno Toll Road sold to San Mateo County;
owner of 7 Mile House, unknown)

1903 - 1909
Egidio Micheli

1909 - 1917
Palmiro Testa

1917 - 1953
Sebastiano Nieri
Lawrence Frugoli

1953 - 1965
Camille and Leonard Stuehler

1965 - 2004
Camille Stuehler and Albert Flynn

2004 - 2011
Vanessa Garcia and Roel Villacarlos

2011 - present
Vanessa Garcia

A c k n o w l e d g MENTS

ORLY AND AIDA AGUSTIN
LOUELLA ALBORNOZ
GIACOMO AND LIA AMADUCCI
JOSE BATILES
WALTER BOLAND
JOE AND STEVEN BOSSO
ROXANA CABALLERO
OLGA CALARZA
BILL CASSIDY
JOHN CHRIST
PALOMA CONCORDIA
MITCH CONLIFFE
CLARKE CONWAY
JOSE FELIX
MARIO GARCIA
DOLORES GOMEZ
BEA GIUSTI
PAUL GREENBAUM
CHRIS HART
BENNY HERNANDEZ
MANNY HERRERA
RICHARD HUERTAS
JAMES JARVIS
BILL LEGASSE
ESTHER LEON
GEMINI AND JOHN MACK

JIMMY AND LORY MARQUEZ
RON LEE MOORE
PAUL AND THELMA PETE
TONY RAGUSIN
DOLORES RODRIGUEZ
TED SAILOR
KENNETH SPROUL
RICK STUEHLER
ANNA SOUTHWICK
LUCILLE STONE
NIKKI STONE
MICHAEL TOMOLA
EUGENE AND ROSELILY VILLACARLOS
JR VILLACARLOS
ROEL VILLACARLOS
LALAINE VILLAMOR
JONI WALKER
JOHN WALSH
MERCEDES VIRZI
TONI ZERNIK

EDIE EPPS *and* RUSSEL MORINE *of Visitacion Valley History Project*
ESTELLE BERTOLUCCI *of San Mateo County Assessor's Office - Recorder's Division*
JEREMY MENZIES *of San Francisco Municipal Transportation Agency*
CHRISTINA MORETTA *of San Francisco Public Library - History Center*
CAROL PETERSON *of San Mateo County History Museum - Historical Association Archives*
THE STAFF OF *California State Library, Sacramento City of Brisbane Public Library CalTrans San Bruno Public Library San Francisco Municipal Transportation Agency*
MICHELLE BAUTE *of San Mateo Public Library*
JOSE ENRIQUE SORIANO *of Fred's Revolucion*

1

STORY STARTS

A TUMBLEWEED WELCOMES A SPECIAL VISITOR, THE LOWLY ORIGINS OF THE 7 MILE HOUSE, ITALIANS GET THINGS STARTED, AND EVERYTHING — AS WE KNOW THUS FAR — IN BETWEEN (1850-1910s)

he only indication that the bar I was about to acquire had any historical value was an old photo on the wall, labeled "The historic Seven Mile House since 1876."

It was a sepia-toned photo of a group of people — men in long, white aprons, their wives, a couple of kids, and presumably, other family members — in front of an old saloon-style sort of structure. "Wines, liquors & cigars," it said on the marquee. "E. Micheli Prop." It didn't look anything like the place we were about to buy, which was a dark dive in the middle of Bayshore Boulevard. It was 2004 and I had agreed to purchase the bar from an elderly, stern-looking woman named Camille Stuehler, without much thought on how to make it work. I just knew I had to. I just knew I could.

Like the tumbleweed that I am, picking up whatever the universe puts in my path, I spent the next couple of years coasting along. I didn't expect that that photo would bring anything meaningful to me, and the hundred-year-old restaurant I was so desperately trying to breathe life back into.

I fostered a love for talking to customers — especially those who used to come in before I took over — and hearing their stories. I was particularly fascinated with hearing how Albert Flynn, who

HOW MANY MORE **STORIES** WERE THERE TO BE TOLD ABOUT **7 MILE HOUSE?** HOW DID THEY FIGURE IN THE FICKLE HISTORY OF SAN FRANCISCO, BRISBANE, AND **SAN MATEO COUNTY**? DID THEY **MATTER** AT ALL?

(Previous page) The Micheli and Testa family. This photo was taken on June 5, 1904, when Egidio's nephew, Leonello Pollini, came to town. You'll read more about that later in this chapter. Man in white shirt and white apron in the middle is Egidio, at his left is partner and brother-in-law Palmiro. The lady in the back holding baby Ecle is Palmiro's wife, Niccola. Little girl in the back is another one of their kids, Eva. (This page) 7 Mile House in 1908. From left: Leonello Pollini, Egidio Micheli, Niccola Testa, Alfio Testa at four or five years old, and Palmiro Testa. "Wheelmen's exchange" was listed as one of Egidio's businesses in the San Francisco-Oakland Directory of 1907.

The Historic <u>Seven Mile House</u> — Past Preserved Into The Future

Dear Friends,

We are fortunate to inherit a piece of the precious past that is Seven Mile House and thank Camille and Al for choosing us as their successors. Rest assured, we intend to preserve this historic beauty and its traditions.

Part of this tradition is to hold its famous barbecue on special occasions. We would like to invite you to gather with old friends at Seven Mile House on **January 29, 2005 at 12 noon**. We'll celebrate being together once again — Seven Mile House-style — one week before the public opening on Superbowl Sunday.

We promise a good old time with some good old friends.

Seven Mile House in the 1940s

Each Seven Mile House customer has an amazing story to tell — tales of the old truck stop, old friendships and more. To preserve these memories, we plan to write a book of anecdotes about customers who have been coming to Seven Mile House for decades. Please keep in touch — we'd love to hear your stories.

"We're fascinated that the historic Seven Mile House has come a long way since the 1800s. We're here to preserve the history in honor of those who always believed in a genuinely good time."
— Roel & Vanessa Villacarlos, Seven Mile House

negotiated 7 Mile's sale with me on behalf of his mother, Camille, ran an illegal sports betting business out of the bar. I loved the notoriety. I loved the mystery. I even gave out a flyer that invited old regulars to come over and share their stories, partly for the purpose of compiling them into a book. That was in 2005.

I loved running my hand across that weirdly slanted wall in the back, wondering why and how the carpenter might have made such a mistake (later I learned it was part of the windmill, which later became a water tank, which they called the "tank house," attached to the main structure). I wondered who had put in the godawful white and green wallpaper that we covered up in the small dining room. When we were moving in, I loved rifling through the drawers and discovering the past owner's "junk"—a coin tray, old key chain

Someday, I told myself, *I'd collect all the old 7 Mile House stories in a book.* Above is a flyer we made to welcome old guests to relive the good ol' times. (Right) An old key wallet, key chain, and coin counter from the previous owner.

BEA GIUSTI'S CONTRIBUTIONS FILLED IN A LARGE GAP IN MY TUMBLEWEED-STYLE RESEARCH, BUT LEFT ME HUNGRY FOR MORE ANSWERS ABOUT 7 MILE HOUSE'S HISTORY.

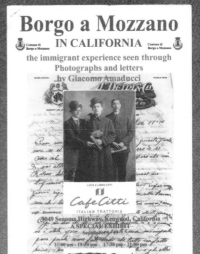

Newspaper clipping (left)

Extended Italian family revels in their momentous reunion

SATURDAY, October 7, 2006

Carolyn Livengood
LIVIN' GOOD

At the turn of the 20th century, Italian immigrants flocked to the San Francisco Bay Area. Groups of young men left their small communities looking for a better future than they could foresee in Italy. Most were in their 20s and untrained but anxious to learn. Men with young families at home came to America to find jobs and housing so they could send for their families to join them.

The immigrants from Anchiano and Borgo a Mozzano in Tuscany were no different. Members of the Micheli family arrived in San Francisco from 1891 through 1907.

At the San Francisco-San Mateo county line, there was a small hotel with a saloon and a "ladies sitting room." Called the 7 Mile House, it was constructed in 1876 and was originally a stagecoach stop. Egidio Micheli purchased the business about 1903 and it soon became the gathering place for immigrants from Anchiano and Borgo a Mozzano.

Micheli encouraged his brother-in-law, Palmiro Testa, a baker who loved to cook, to work with him in the restaurant. Both men also enjoyed rolling cigars, which became a big business at the restaurant.

On June 5, 1904, a photograph was taken of this group of immigrants in front of the 7 Mile House. That photograph still hangs in the restaurant located at 2800 Bayshore Blvd. at Geneva Avenue in Brisbane.

After six years in the hotel and restaurant business, Micheli left to open a cigar and tobacco store on Grant Avenue in San Francisco. Testa bought the 7 Mile House; he tended bar and both he and his wife, Nicola, cooked. Nine young men were living in the hotel and a few worked as waiters. Testa

sold the business in 1917 when he moved to Santa Rosa and opened a cigar and tobacco store on Fourth Street.

Fifteen descendants of Micheli and Testa met at the 7 Mile House on Sept. 17 to hold their first reunion. Although some had met before, they were all meeting, for the first time, their cousins, Lia and Giacomo Amaducci visiting from Borgo a Mozzano.

The other descendants, ranging in age from 3 to 87, were: Margot and George Giusti and Karen and Bill Giusti, both couples from San Bruno; Aldo and Glen Giusti of Santa Rosa; Joy Testa, Bill Neads, and Paula Friday, all of Vallejo; Steve Giusti and Matthew Giusti of Mountain View; and Bea and Silvio Giusti of Mill Valley.

"Giacomo Amaducci, a professor of history and art in Italy, and his wife collect old family photographs and promptly requested a new group photo be taken in front of the 7 Mile House," said Bea, who does genealogy. She traded information with Giacomo, organized the reunion, and supplied the history for this article. "We all insisted that the current owners, Vanessa and Roel Villacarlos, join us in the photo.

"Afterwards, we all sat down and enjoyed the beautifully presented food in the dining room which was formerly the 'ladies sitting room.' The hotel at the 7 Mile House is gone and the restaurant is now a sports bar, but on the sides of the building, you can still see the original wood building."

"Photographs of the earlier building will soon adorn the walls of the dining room," said Vanessa. "This has been very exciting for Roel and me to meet the descendants of two former owners of our 7 Mile House and to share in this 'once in a lifetime' event."

San Mateo County Times
CLOSER TO HOME™

Carolyn Livengood
News Correspondent

140 Sheryl Dr
San Bruno, CA 94066-1
Phone: (650) 355-5
Fax: (650) 355-55
carolynlivengood@sanbrunocable.c

SanMateoCountyTimes.com
an ANG Newspaper

(right)

Borgo a Mozzano
IN CALIFORNIA
the immigrant experience seen through Photographs and letters
by Giacomo Amaducci

The descendants of the first verifiable owners of 7 Mile House had a reunion in 2006. It was worthy enough to be in the papers (left). Later, they mounted a photographic exhibition in Kenwood, California (above).

---

wallets, cups for Liar's Dice. I threw nothing away. How many more stories were there to be told about 7 Mile? How did they all figure in the fickle history of San Francisco, San Mateo County, or even California? Did they matter much at all? I collected and absorbed whatever I could about the place.

The book plans progressed very slowly, until one day in 2006. While I was tending bar, a woman by the name of Bea Giusti came into 7 Mile and saw the old photo. "I know this picture!" she said. She was a genealogist, one who had actively been researching her family's history. "This is my ancestor's bar!" E. Micheli, proprietor of the 7 Mile House, was her great granduncle. That visit led to a family reunion in 7 Mile House that year, and a family photo exhibit, albeit in another venue, in 2007.

Bea's contributions filled in a large gap in my tumbleweed-style research, but left me hungry for more answers about 7 Mile House's history. Twelve years after I first put out that flyer, I believe I have most of them.

Egidio Micheli's, and later, Palmiro Testa's 7 Mile House was quite successful. Later in
this chapter, you will read that they added a "ladies' sitting room" (advertised by a sign
jutting out from the side of the building), and sold cigars that they rolled themselves. They
also sold Milwaukee Steam & Golden State Beer—a pre-cursor of craft beers today.

Bea said the photo was incorrectly labeled, as Egidio Micheli bought the property in 1903. Whoever labeled it might have been referring to an old article in "Early Inns and Roadhouses: A History of Hospitality in San Mateo County," a collection of essays culled together in the 1970s. One of the essays mentions that "Seven Mile House…remains relatively unchanged since its construction in 1876" (more on this later). In another essay in the same collection, it was mentioned that "as the stagecoach passed over the county line on El Camino Real in what is now Daly City, the first mile house it stopped at was Seven Mile. The first mention of this place is in the County Assessor's book of 1853."

I had attributed *that* as *our* 7 Mile House. I even threw a 160th year birthday bash for the restaurant in 2013. Later, as earnest research for this book began, I realized my mistake, since Bayshore Boulevard was and never will be El Camino Real.

The discovery of gold in the foothills of Sierra Nevada in 1848 brought people flocking to California. A popular port of entry was San Francisco, which greeted travelers from all over the world by boat, foot, and wagon. The city of San Francisco grew at a rate of two thousand people a month. This is San Francisco Harbor in 1851.

Portsmouth Square, from where John W. Whistman launched his omnibus service.

OMNIBUS : 1. Omnibus à trois chevaux; 2. Omnibus de chemin de fer, à chevaux; 3. Omnibus de famille, à chevaux; 4. Omnibus d'hôtel, automobile.

The omnibus was basically benches on wheels, offering no comfort except the shorter travel time between two points. (Opposite page) An approximation of where the mile houses (including the 7 Mile House in San Francisco) stood during the first half of the century. The red line represents the train route of the Bayshore Cutoff, which started construction in 1906; the yellow line shows the San Francisco and San Jose Railroad, which started in 1864.

The farthest point from which I could start digging was the mid-19th century. This was when the Gold Rush happened, and when California officially became part of the United States. I made headway when I began looking at how roads were built throughout Northern California, and the gruelling experience of travel back then.

First, there was the traffic—or what they might have considered traffic in those days. The discovery of gold at the foothills of Sierra Nevada in 1848 brought on a horde at the start of 1849, with thousands of fortune seekers streaming in California from all over—from Asia, Latin America, and within the United States by boat, foot, and wagon. Before this, the main destinations were the

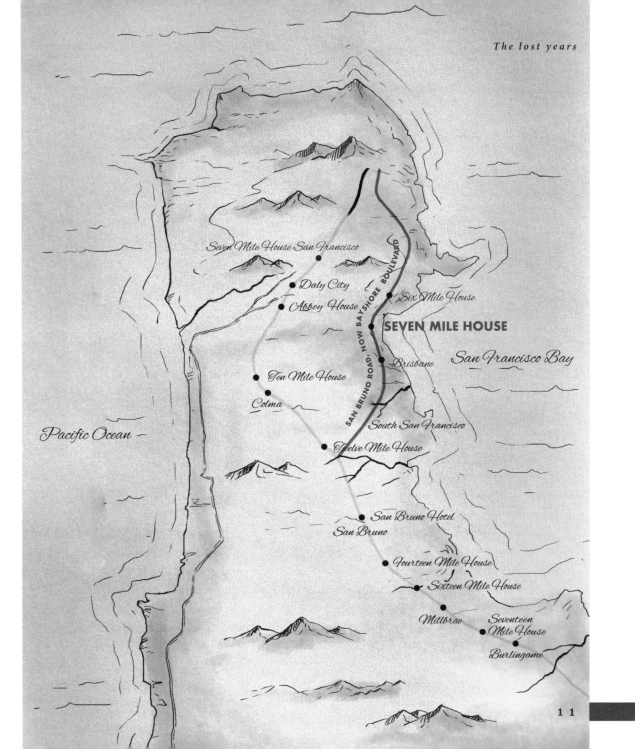

Seven Mile House San Francisco

Daly City

Abbey House

Six Mile House

SAN BRUNO ROAD, NOW BAYSHORE BOULEVARD

SEVEN MILE HOUSE

Brisbane

San Francisco Bay

Ten Mile House

Colma

South San Francisco

Twelve Mile House

Pacific Ocean —

San Bruno Hotel

San Bruno

Fourteen Mile House

Sixteen Mile House

Millbrae

Seventeen Mile House

Burlingame

WHO LAID THE FOUNDATION FOR THE
7 MILE HOUSE?

DAVID S. (OR D.S.) COOK

was one of the earliest settlers in San Mateo County. He opened San Mateo House with Nicholas de Peyster (spelled Dupeyster in some documents) in 1852, which he expanded with a large frame building brought in different parts on eight different ships. The shrewd Mr. Cook bought out de Peyster in 1856 and continued to deal mightily in real estate till his death.

SIMON M. MEZES

was once described as "one of those typical grandees of Old Spain," having come to California from Puerto Rico, where, at the age of twenty-one, he had already headed the largest bank on the island. He arrived in the States in 1850, organized a legal firm to distribute ranchos for the Spanish, and was one of the original patentees of Rancho de las Pulgas. He rose to great political influence, particularly in Redwood City, which was first named Mezesville. He demanded that it be changed due to his aversion to publicity.

HORACE HAWES

was born in poverty in New York— he was even given in servitude as a boy to a nearby family, from which he bought his freedom after four years. Mental and physical grit brought him to the world of politics in the east coast, and later in San Francisco, where, from 1849 to 1871, he served two terms as an assemblyman and one as a senator. He devoted his legislative life to service of the people.

missions, which were scattered all over the state. After, all roads led to the city of San Francisco, whose population grew at a rate of two thousand people a month.

Second, there was the absence of comfort, and the exorbitant costs. Whether or not the travelers came over land or sea, the travel was long, arduous, and expensive. A certain John W. Whistman had put up an erratically scheduled stagecoach service that started in San Francisco Plaza (or Portsmouth Square, near today's Chinatown in San Francisco) to San Jose, which was then expected to become the state's capital. He used an old French omnibus—basically benches with wheels, no shocks, no springs, no nothing—which was pulled by a few mules and half-wild mustangs. If the weather was fair, the omnibus cut down travel time to nine hours (compared to a day's walk), but riders got their fair share of bruised buttocks from being bounced about on rough roads. The fare wasn't cheap. Pre-gold rush, everything could be paid for in cattle hides. But when gold was discovered, everything was a "pinch" or an "ounce." The fare for a stagecoach ride was two ounces of gold, or twenty-

A SCENIC ROUTE

Though humble, the San Bruno Toll Road received some exposure in the press. On April 30, 1859, when it was already being used for travel, the San Mateo *Gazette* describes:

"...The landscape is indeed beautiful—the traveler finds no cold winds or chilling fogs—no sand through which his roadsters drag their weary feet, but with a firm footing, a carriageway smooth, but built mostly of broken rock, a road comparatively level, he glides along at a 2:40 pace, and finds himself in full view of the City of Hills before he fairly dream San Bruno lies behind him. The road is in some places rather narrow, where it has been cut through the rocks, and it has some short and abrupt angles, but the company are preparing to remedy these defects, and very soon the road will be the safest, as it is now the most pleasant in the country..."

four to thirty-two dollars (or around $670 and $900 in 2017). Winter travel was worse, when the ice became mud and stuck to the horses, wheels, and passenger's clothes.

One of the most favored routes then was the west side of San Bruno Mountain on El Camino Real ("The King's Highway" or "The Royal Road"). This was established in the 1770s and served as the main thoroughfare from Mission Dolores (or Mission San Francisco de Asis) in the north of the peninsula, to Mission Sta. Clara in the south. But the gravitational pull of San Francisco brought about the possibility of carving a more straightforward route from the east side of San Bruno Mountain. This side faced the bay; the other side faced the Pacific Ocean.

Three enterprising men were up to task: David S. Cook, Horace Hawes, and Simon Mezes. Work on the San Bruno Road commenced in 1858. To help finance the endeavor, a toll was to be charged to cover the costs of hiring a workforce, hauling gravel and dirt to fill in the marshes, constructing a drawbridge to cross San Bruno Canal, and diverting creeks into culverts. The three men secured a franchise for the operation of a toll road from State Legislature in Sacramento, and thus began construction of a main thoroughfare that was situated along what is now the northern city limits of Brisbane. It started from El Camino Real (current day San Mateo Avenue), continued straight through South San Francisco, crossed what was known as "the slough" or Colma Creek on a drawbridge, and onto the part of San Bruno Toll Road that is now known as Bayshore Boulevard.

The road wasn't much to look at in the beginning; it was wide enough in some parts to accommodate two wagons,

A drive to the corner of Geneva Avenue and Carter Street near Cow Palace reveals a street sign that bears Geneva's former name: Walbridge, after Ohio native Hiram Walbridge, original owner of the land on which 7 Mile House now stands. Brisbane Mayor Clarke Conway told me about the existence of this street sign, and I had to see it for myself. Let's hope vandals don't tear it down or deface it in any way, as it is a historic landmark in its own right.

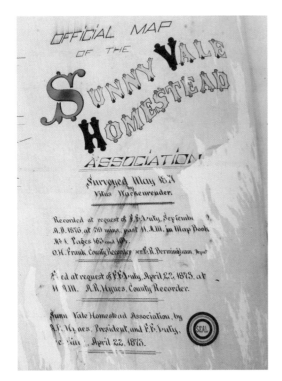

COOK, HAWES, AND MEZES SECURED A **FRANCHISE** FROM STATE LEGISLATURE IN **SACRAMENTO** FOR THE **OPERATION OF A TOOL BOOTH**, AND THUS BEGAN CONSTRUCTION OF A MAIN THOROUGHFARE ALONG WHAT IS NOW THE **NORTHERN CITY LIMITS OF BRISBANE.**

Title section of Sunnyvale Homestead Association map, which shows where the toll gate is located (next page).

and wound on a narrow stretch of earth that was still close enough to the sea to be lapped by waves. Landfills were decades into the future, so the edge of the road still had sand and shell mounds that scrunched beneath the feet and wheels.

According to San Mateo County historian Darold Fredricks in one of his articles for *The Daily Journal*, as the road was built in 1858 to 1859, a little structure was put up to serve as a toll gate. No one called it a roadhouse or an inn yet. It would be just over ten years till this little spot in the middle of nowhere would be mentioned in the papers again, and called by the name it carries till this day: a mile house—the 7 Mile House, to be exact.

In different documents from the 1870s, 7 Mile was used only to refer to a location: in a tiny announcement in the *Daily Alta California* newspaper on July 17, 1870, Market Inspector S.B.

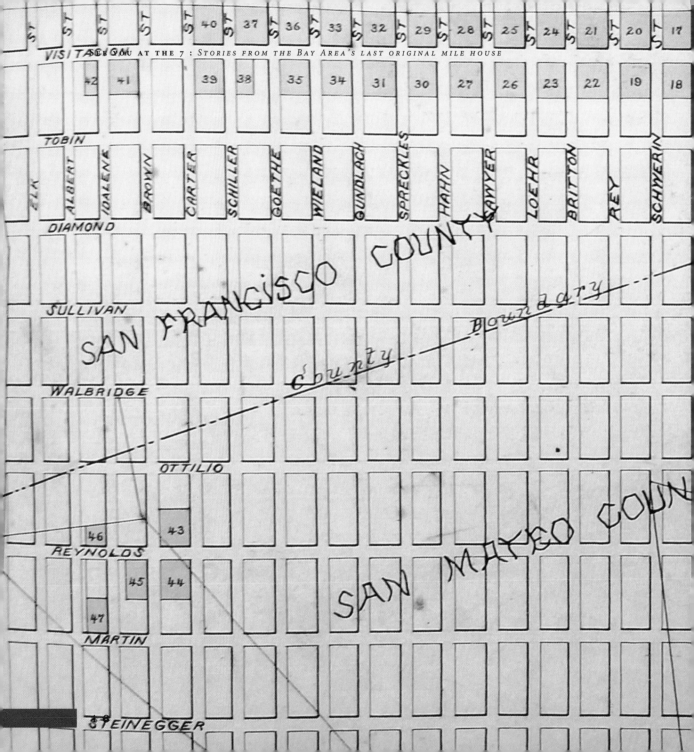

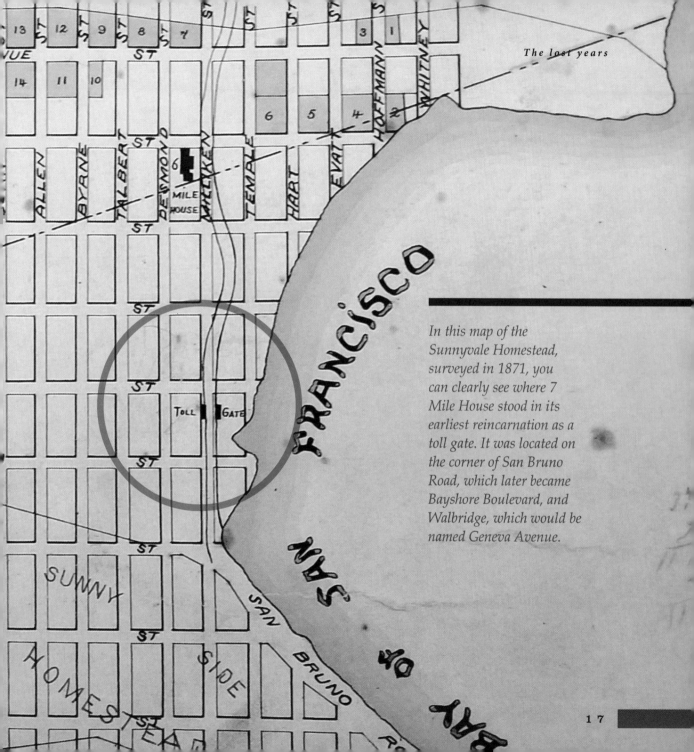

In this map of the
Sunnyvale Homestead,
surveyed in 1871, you
can clearly see where 7
Mile House stood in its
earliest reincarnation as a
toll gate. It was located on
the corner of San Bruno
Road, which later became
Bayshore Boulevard, and
Walbridge, which would be
named Geneva Avenue.

(Left) The Seven Mile House Tract was mentioned in the San Mateo County Properties Assessment Book of 1877-1878 to describe the delineation of the land owned by the Visitacion Land Company. (Below) A clerk named William J. H. Bewley is listed as living in Seven Mile House on San Bruno Road in 1871.

William Ralston, co-founder of the Bank of California, chose the 7 Mile House as a horse-changing station for "Ralston's Tally-Ho." This was part of a flamboyant stunt to celebrate his bank's fifth anniversary, in which he raced a train carrying his guests from San Francisco to his mansion in Belmont.

Bookstaver was quoted denying that thirty-five heads of cattle "near Seven Mile House" had died of disease. In a San Francisco Directory for 1871, a certain William J.H. Bewley is listed as "clerk" for 7 Mile House along San Bruno Road. In an 1873 map of the Sunny Vale Homestead, a little box labeled "toll gate" is clearly etched out along the San Bruno Road, on the corner of modern-day Bayshore and Geneva (formerly Walbridge). In the San Mateo County Property Assessor's Book of 1877-1878, it's mentioned as "Seven Mile House Tract" to delineate part of the area belonging to the Visitacion Land Company. There *is* a tale that puts 7 Mile House in a less dreary light, however. It goes like this:

William Ralston, who founded Bank of California along with D.O. Mills, wanted to celebrate his bank's fifth anniversary in 1869 in a spectacular way. Ralston was known to be eccentric and extravagant, so instead of holding it at a hotel, he convinced his partner that a party on a train ride from San Francisco to Belmont would be much more exciting. It would be capped with another party at Ralston's estate in Canada de Diablo, which originally belonged to an Italian count. This sounded fairly sane—until Ralston said he wanted to race the train from point to point with a horse-driven carriage. This stunt was thereafter known as "Ralston's Tally-Ho," and used the mile houses as relay stations to change horses. It was an elaborate stunt, but Ralston had the means and the money. The 7 Mile House was one of his changing stations, the second out of six stops, and Howard's Place his last, for a total of thirty-four miles. As expected, he beat the train. Tally-Ho makes for a heart-stopping narrative, good enough for Hollywood, but during those days, it was met by criticism by the frugal-minded.

In 1889, Cook, Hawes, and Mezes sold the road to San Mateo County, and 7 Mile House began its long and infamous journey as a destination for, well, people who like to have just too much fun.

Records that reveal who owned 7 Mile in the late 19th century have yet to be discovered, but whoever it was certainly made architectural improvements—most likely in 1876, as mentioned in

11

ACTED ONLY AS A COMMISSIONER.

DEFENSE OF A POOL SELLER.

TRIED BEFORE A SAUSALITO JURY.

A Dog Fight Which May Lead to Trouble for the Spectators.

Special Dispatches to the Chronicle.

SAUSALITO, July 27.—The case involving the pool-sellers of Sausalito was tried to-day in the Recorder's court. The defendant was J. M. McGee, an employe of Corbett & Co., and the prosecuting witness Marshal J. E. Creed.

The evidence for the people showed that the defendant had accepted $1 from Creed for a ticket on a certain horse in a certain race. The defense claimed that the accused had taken the money as a commissioner for Goldtree & Co., who are running poolrooms at the Seven-mile House in San Mateo county.

The Recorder charged the jury to the effect that it was immaterial whether McGee was the principal or agent. Thomas P. Boyd, City Attorney of San Rafael, appeared for the defendants. The prosecution was conducted by A. Silva, the Town Attorney.

The jury, composed of Commodore Harrison, William N. Ketcham, Captain William Barrowe, George Tashiera, Con O'Leary, John Thomas, W. H. Herald, William Getchier, Peter Claudianos, G. Stahl, John Mason and William Ritchie, went out at 7 o'clock and at midnight had not agreed on a verdict.

AUTOMOBILE IS OBSTREPEROUS.

C. L. Fair Has a Mishap Near the Seven-Mile House.

Charles L. Fair is getting a world of experience as an automobile driver. He has not mastered the idiosyncrasies of his horseless vehicle as yet, but he is learning rapidly by experience. His latest accident occurred yesterday while he was spinning along the county road in the neighborhood of the Seven-Mile House with his wife. The automobile is said to have become obstreperous at a critical moment and unpleasant things happened. Fortunately no one was seriously hurt, but Fair and his wife are said to have both suffered from fright. It is said that experience is the only thing that can properly tutor a man in the gentle art of handling an automobile, and Fair is busily engaged just now in getting the experience.

NOVEMBER 9. 1901.

POLICE ARREST A BAY PIRATE

Exciting Chase Out by by the Seven-Mile House.

Band of Thieves Loots Large Quantity of White Paint.

Numerous complaints have been sent to police headquarters of the operations of a gang of bay pirates who have been stealing goods from vessels in the bay. Captain Seymour detailed Detective Crockett on the case, and Thursday he got a clew in the shape of a strange sloop that was seen going in the direction of Mission Bay. He was also able to discover that three men were in the habit of hiring a wagon from Lambert's stables at Fifth and Folsom streets.

Crockett stationed himself in a house near the stables and shortly after dawn yesterday morning he saw two men drive out of the stables with a wagon. He quickly hired a buggy and trailed behind them till they reached the beach near the Seven-mile House, San Bruno road. The men had stolen a large quantity of white paint from a schooner lying at Third and Kentucky streets. It belonged to W. P. Fuller & Co. They had loaded the paint into the sloop and sailed with it to Mission Bay, where they unloaded it Thursday night and piled it on the beach near the Seven-mile House.

Crockett watched them till they began loading the paint into the wagon and he telephoned to the Potrero station for Policeman Ennis. As soon as Ennis arrived they advanced upon the pirates, who saw them coming and jumped into the wagon, driving off furiously. They drove against a fence and jumped off. Crockett fired a shot at one of them. He chased another of the gang through pig pens and sloughs till he overtook him and soon had the handcuffs on him. The other two escaped.

The captured pirate gave his name as John Reed. He had a revolver in his pocket, and when the officers went to the sloop they found another loaded revolver and a dark lantern. The white lead was marked "A. R." which is W. P. Fuller & Co.'s private mark. Crockett and Ennis loaded the wagon and Crockett drove into the city with it and his prisoner, while Ennis remained to keep guard over the sloop. Reed was placed in "the tanks." A search will be made for his two confederates.

Poolrooms, vehicular accidents, and pirate sightings and arrests were all par for the course in and around 7 Mile House.

the "Early Inns and Roadhouses" essay. A clipping from the San Francisco *Chronicle* dated July 28, 1896 mentions poolrooms were being run out of 7 Mile by Goldtree and Co. (While there were two other 7 Mile Houses nearby that were mentioned repeatedly in other clippings from that period, this one was the only one specified to be located in San Mateo County; the others were in San Francisco County and Berkeley.) Three years after, San Bruno Road seems to have had some upgrades from

In 1898, a young man named Egidio Micheli boarded a ship in Genoa and sailed to Ellis Island. He was twenty-four years old, around five foot nine, with black hair and grey eyes. He was going to the States to join his brother, Guglielmo, who had a wood and coal business in San Francisco. He worked as a driver, and in 1903 became an entrepreneur when he bought the 7 Mile House, which, his descendant Bea Giusti says, "was a saloon, restaurant, and hotel located just south of San Francisco."

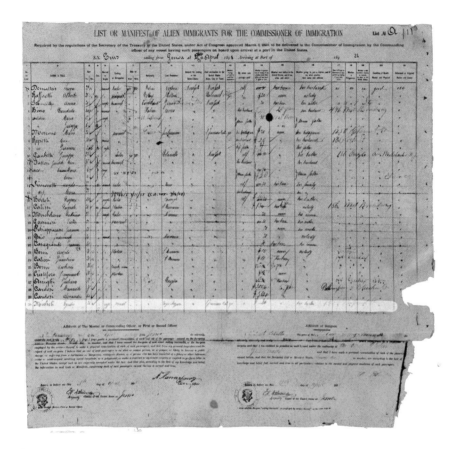

The passenger manifest from the *S.S. Ems* lists Egidio Micheli as a merchant. He entered New York City on May 11, 1898.

being buggy-only to car-worthy as well, as one Charles L. Fair got into an automobile mishap near 7 Mile due to the "obstreperousness" of his vehicle. 7 Mile appears in the news again in 1901, when a detective trailed bay pirates to the roadhouse, in front of which they had buried their loot on the beach (nothing to be excited about, though—the "treasure" was "a large quantity of white paint [belonging to] W.P. Fuller and Co."). A chase ensued and ended with the capture of pirate John Reed, who was then placed in "the tanks." Maybe he sold them to a 19th-century version of Home Depot? We don't know.

Around the time sailors and butchers and tanners and other hardworking folk were dropping

The handwritten deed that passed on the lot on the corner of Geneva (formerly Walbridge) and Bayshore in 1903. It was from Isabella Walbridge, an heiress from Ohio and daughter of the aforementioned Hiram, to Giuseppi Lercari of San Francisco.

This was taken around 1910 or 1911, the same day as the photo featured on page eight. In the back, you'll notice the windmill tower, which explains the slanted wall behind our current-day storage area and office. In the front row, seated are: Alfio Testa, his father Palmiro, mother Niccola, and sister Ecle. The young lady with her hands on Palmiro's shoulders is his daughter, Eva.

in 7 Mile for a round of pool, its first verifiable owner was disembarking the *S.S. Ems* in New York City from Genoa, Italy. It was May 11, 1898. Thanks to Bea Giusti, we are privy to several details of Papa Egidio's arrival and life in the U.S.: Egidio Micheli was listed as a merchant, and his papers also stated that he had previously been in the U.S. for five years. Then twenty-four years old, the bright-eyed Egidio planned to travel to San Francisco to see his brother, Guglielmo Micheli, who was in the wood and coal business. Later, Egidio joined him as a driver, and stayed with Guglielmo and guar.; tuition earned while learning. Moler's System of Colleges, 642-644 Clay st.

MEN to learn barber trade; situations guaranteed. S. F. Barber College, 741 Howard st.

WANTED—Feeder on folding, box cutting and creasing press. 520 Market st.

YOUNG boy to learn horseshoeing. Hoppe's blacksmith, 7-Mile House, San Bruno road.

WANTED—Steady, clean lunchman in restaurant. 111 Larkin st.

YOUNG man for photo supply house; must understand photography. Box 9331, Call.

SAILORS, ordinary seamen, for Sound, south coast, New York, Europe. Lane's, 504 Davis.

PENSION atty.. E. A. Bullis. r. 40. Phelan bld

7 MILE HOUSE BECAME A FAVORITE MEETING PLACE FOR ITALIAN IMMIGRANTS, AND HUB FOR BUSINESSMEN AND THOSE SEEKING PROTEGÉS.

sister-in-law in their apartment on Dupont Street (now Grant Avenue). Eventually, Egidio moved into an apartment on Broadway Street. By 1902, he had joined a certain L. Giovanni & Co. for his own coal business.

In about 1903, presumably liquid with earnings from the coal trade, Egidio bought the 7 Mile House, which was a saloon, restaurant, and hotel south of San Francisco. Soon, it became a favorite meeting place for immigrants from Anchiano and his native Borgo a Mozzano in Tuscany, Italy. His sister, Niccola was married to a baker named Palmiro Testa, whom Egidio took in as a partner at 7 Mile. Palmiro became the cook, and during his off-hours, he and Egidio would roll cigars, a pastime they enjoyed immensely.

Around this time, the land on which 7 Mile House was located also switched hands—Isabella Walbridge, an heiress from Ohio, sold it to Giuseppi Lercari of San Francisco on February 17, 1903 for $2,500.

On June 4, 1904, Egidio's nephew Leonello Pollini, who was nineteen at the time, arrived from Italy. The next day, there was a big party to welcome young Leonello to San Francisco. Uncles, aunts, cousins, and friends from Borgo a Mozzano gathered at the 7. This event is the one captured in the famed photograph that hangs in the 7 Mile House today. In a letter to his family in Italy dated June 6, 1904, he said he had gone directly to the restaurant, where he saw Uncle Egidio Micheli's shop. "(I)

7 MILE
HIDDEN BEHIND
STRUCTURE

A long shot of the Bayshore in 1909 shows how isolated 7 Mile House was,
making it an ideal area for surreptitious and suspicious activity.

met Niccola, Palmiro, Eva, Ugo (Egidio's younger brother), Guglielmo, (and other relatives) Adamo, Carlo della Mea, Raffaello Bandiera," the young man wrote. "Uncle Egidio has set up a pavilion where you can dance and because of lots of people went there, they were obliged to sell them food. People drink a lot of beer."

By all accounts, business was booming. The cigars that Egidio and Palmiro rolled in their spare time eventually became big business for 7 Mile. The saloon grew, and a "ladies sitting room" was added to the building to accommodate women. The restaurant even became a hub for freelancers of sorts—

Whenever 7 Mile House would appear in the papers, it would most often be about crime and accidents. Clippings from the San Francisco *Chronicle* (from left): a clamdigger is robbed in 1902, hold ups in 1910, and a man selling thinned milk in 1908. What a difference a century and a half can make!

an ad that appeared in 1905 in the San Francisco *Call* asked for a "young boy who wanted to learn horseshoeing" should drop by "Hoppe's blacksmith at 7-Mile House, San Bruno Road."

But then, there was crime. Always crime. Perhaps it was because of the influx of strangers due to the newly constructed railroad cut-off at the San Bruno Mountain, or the restaurant's location, which was largely isolated, and the general lawless atmosphere of San Mateo County. The 7 Mile House was a frequent target of hold-ups and robberies, a few occurring in broad daylight. It was residence to some scoundrels too, such as boarder Joseph Kennel, who was arrested for selling thinned milk in 1908.

Leonello returned to Italy after a while, but came back to the U.S. in 1909. By then, Egidio—who had married Genoan Balsamina Giorgi—had sold his 7 Mile shares to Palmiro. Egidio moved on to the cigar and tobacco business with Angelino Petri and formed A. Petri & Company. The store was located at 1461-1463 Grant Ave., while the factory was at 55-57 Brannan Place. Egidio and Balsamina moved back to Italy shortly after. In 1947, 7 Mile's first known owner passed away in Borgo a Mozzano. Both he and Balsamina are buried in the family chapel in Anchiano.

*Railyard workers in 1900. This photo was taken across the street from
7 Mile House. (San Francisco Trains, Ralph Dominici collection)*

While running the business, Palmiro, his family, and ten boarders, lived at the 7 Mile House. It was then listed to be at No. 7 San Bruno Road, San Mateo County. Leonello moved in as well, and helped staff the bar and restaurant. Niccola took over the kitchen. During his seven years as a saloon keeper, Palmiro got into a couple of relatively high-profile scrapes, which you'll read about in the next chapter.

The reputation of 7 Mile House as headquarters to notorious characters with hearts of gold, and whose barks were worse than their bites, was born.

(Left) Men dropping in for a drink at 7 Mile House in the 1900s. (Below) As Visitacion Valley poised for development in the first decade of the 1900s, so too did 7 Mile House's business grow. In this infograph, you can see the lot where the bar is located, next to California (now Pacific) Gas & Electric Corporation.

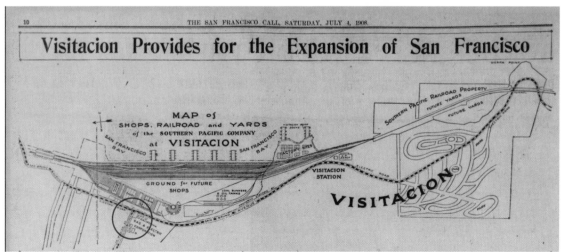

10   THE SAN FRANCISCO CALL, SATURDAY, JULY 4, 1908.

Visitacion Provides for the Expansion of San Francisco

Inside 7 Mile House. Behind the bar is Egidio Micheli and Palmiro Testa. The lady standing on the left is Eva Testa, Palmiro's daughter. On her left is her future husband, Donald Day.

Placing the MILE HOUSES

Peninsula mile houses were a by-product of the Gold Rush. Travelers needed a respite during their difficult rides, and so these roadhouses were built as rest areas, pubs, wheel exchange stops, stores which sold a few items in limited supply, or "hotels"—which were mostly spaces where one could roll out his rucksack and get some shuteye. Some were mere farm houses and shacks, and some were grand affairs, such as the One Mile House or Abbey House, which was owned by mobster Chris Lilly, and Nicholas de Peyster's Half Way or San Mateo House.

It's come to be accepted that mile houses were so named according to their distances from the San Francisco Ferry Building or the Embarcadero. Considering, however, that the Ferry Building was built in 1896, much later than the mile houses were, this theory is incorrect. More plausible is that they were named for their distance from Portsmouth Square, where Whistman first launched his stagecoaches.

James Jarvis of historical drinking society E Clampus Vitus concurs. "Portsmouth Square, also called 'The Plaza' in the 1800s, was the heart of San Francisco, indeed the oldest part of the city itself," he says. "Located between Chinatown and the Financial District, Portsmouth Square was where City Hall was located, along with the main Post Office, both from the 1850s. Listings for 5 Mile House (in old) SF City Directories say, '5 Mile House - 5 Miles from the Plaza'. This almost certainly confirms my theory."

Windmills at Four Mile House, Bay View ©1957 N. Blair

A panoramic photo shows both the 6 Mile House and 7 Mile House on San Bruno Toll Road in the late 1910s or early 1920s. This area once thrived with railyard activity. Now, it's all vacant land.

6 MILE HOUSE

············
WILD
THINGS,
WILD
TIMES

7 *MILE HOUSE SURVIVES PROHIBITION, PALMIRO TESTA'S ADVENTUROUS STREAK, NEW OWNERS TAKE OVER, AND CAMILLE AND LENNY STUEHLER ENTER THE PICTURE (1909-LATE 1940s)*

There were several times during the research of this book that my cousin, a writer and editor who helped me organize my thoughts, had to pull me back from delving too much into Albert Flynn's involvement in illegal bookmaking.

For those unaware, Albert "Al" Flynn was Camille Stuehler's older son, from whom I bought 7 Mile House in 2004. Al helped his mother manage 7 Mile House when she had grown too old to work full time. I met Al a few times to talk about the turnover of the bar; he was a nice old man — tall, likely good-looking in his youth — who was visibly suffering from health issues. Al's foray into bookmaking led him to being top man for Ronald "The Cigar" Sacco's Northern California operations — which earned him a federal indictment in 2000. Indicted along with him were Bobby Riggs, Jr. (not to be mistaken for the tennis player), and Armando Nardi, both of whom make cameo appearances later in this book. It was believed that one of the toll-free numbers used in making bets originated from a phone booth in 7 Mile House. In gambling circles, Ron Sacco is considered the "godfather of sports betting," and the man that "made the entire offshore gambling industry possible," according to online betting enthusiasts.

"This is the story of 7 Mile," my cousin would remind me. "Not about Al Flynn's illegal

(Previous page) Bayshore streetview circa 1910 and 2017. (This page) A partial view of the three cities: San Francisco, Daly City, and Brisbane, looking southwest from Little Hollywood. This shows Southern Pacific railyard in its prime in the 1930s. These days, that same land is barren.

SOUTHERN PACIFIC RAILYARD

7 MILE HOUSE

THE RISK-TAKING SPIRIT AT **7 MILE** DIDN'T START WITH **AL FLYNN**. THAT HONOR GOES TO **PALMIRO TESTA**, TO WHOM **EGIDIO** HANDED OVER THE 7 MILE HOUSE IN 1909.

More treasures found in old drawers: an old rotary phone; matchboxes bearing the restaurant's phone number (still the same after all these years) and old address; and an old dollar bill, whose edges have been eaten away by time.

Palmiro Testa, 7 Mile House's second known owner, during a portrait session in a Boston studio in 1893.

21 WEST ST.
BOSTON.

A page from the 1920 Census shows Palmiro and his family as residents of Santa Rosa, Sonoma County. He was fifty years old at the time; he was naturalized in 1906.

activities. That can be your next book."

I admit, I'm drawn to the illicitness of it all: How did the phone calls go? How'd they collect the money? Where did they put it? How does one even *attempt* to get into something that might get you arrested? It was all such a contrast to my sunny, almost painfully naive upbringing in the Philippines.

When I meet people, I immediately assume they're good. This is the way I approach people

ACQUITTED OF GAMBLING.

BURLINGAME, October 22.—Peter
Testa, proprietor of the "Seven-Mile
House" in the Visitacion valley, was
today acquitted of a gambling charge
by a jury in Justice Porter E. Lamb's
court. Testa has been cited to show
cause why his liquor license should
not be revoked.

On October 24, 1914, Palmiro appeared in a small item in the San Francisco *Chronicle* about being acquitted of running an illegal gambling operation in the outhouse behind 7 Mile. The charge cost him his liquor license. A more detailed story appeared three days later in the same paper.

at 7 Mile: *You're a good person. Let me serve you.* Everyone starts off with a blank slate. I sincerely feel let down when people show their bad side, cause trouble, or disrespect the staff. I hate to kick people out, but I've done it, because I also believe that if you invite bad elements into the business, then more damage will follow. Not that I'm saying Al was bad (time and again, in all the interviews conducted for this book, everyone who knew him extolled his warmth and generosity). On the contrary—and legal issues aside—I think I would've gotten along with the man. I'm riveted by and respect his audacity.

But events and intentions do carry respective consequences, and I think that a person should take those consequences as opportunities to learn to be better.

The risk-taking spirit at 7 Mile didn't start with Al Flynn, though. That honor goes to Palmiro Testa, to whom Egidio handed over the 7 Mile House in 1909.

Palmiro, like Egidio, was from Borgo a Mozzano. He was born on Easter Sunday, March 21, 1869, and arrived in the United States on the S.S. *Kaiser Wilhelm II* on February 27, 1893. His destination was Boston, and in the ship's manifest, he stated he was a baker.

By 1909, Palmiro had taken on the Americanized nickname "Peter," and appeared in the news for running a gambling operation in the outhouse behind 7 Mile. He and the notorious "Beefsteak Bill" Markt, who ran Real Thing saloon, got equal billing in an item about being the focus of several raids over the weeks leading up to October 27, 1914. The story says the bail money for the gamblers was handed over by no less than a police sergeant, and that two detectives who visited Real Thing were severely beaten up. One can only assume that Peter, like many other business owners during

GANGSTERS,
business, and POLITICS,
in San Mateo County

BILLY MULLIGAN.

angsterism wasn't anything new in San Mateo. It's been said that San Mateo County was "born in scandal," beginning when New York native David Broderick set his political sights on San Francisco in 1852, and lost due to the maneuverings of Senator William Gwin, who led the southern states. Disillusioned, Broderick resorted to more familiar ways—that is, the ways of the streets of New York. His disenchantment with "respectable folk" was enough that he turned to a less genteel crowd for support.

One of Broderick's most loyal henchmen was Billy Mulligan, who was also friends with gangsters Chris Lilly and Yankee Sullivan. Other members of Broderick's cadre were David Scannell and James Casey. But these men weren't ordinary goons. They dressed sharply, owned businesses (even a newspaper), and held down positions of power. By stuffing ballot boxes and through intimidation, this group of men and their ilk held sway over politics and business in San Mateo and San Francisco.

This all came to a denouement when the major players in Broderick's clique had either been executed, committed suicide, or deported by the San Francisco Vigilance Committee of 1856. John Hittell, pioneer and historian of early California, wrote: "The professional criminals, as a class, fled in terror."

This is not to mean the county—nor the state—was cleansed of criminal activity. Many complicated and multi-layered intrigues were to follow through the decades, which make other compelling tales altogether.

those days, had some connection to the mobsters that controlled commerce and much of politics in the Bay Area.

While Peter was acquitted for gambling, his liquor license was revoked, and it was ruled that 7 Mile House and Real Thing be closed at once.

We'll never know for sure, but maybe it was this incident that moved Peter to lie low and prepare for a quieter future. On November 6, 1914, a small news announcement was published about Peter transferring his Byrne Street property to his wife Niccola, and in 1917, he bade the saloon scene goodbye and opened a cigar shop on Fourth Street in Sta. Rosa, California. He died at the age of eighty-seven on Christmas Eve in 1956, and is buried in the Santa Rosa Memorial Park.

When 7 Mile resurfaces in the news after the property transfer, it's for nobler reasons. A fire had gutted the home of one Pera family in Visitacion Valley, and the community rallied around to help. "The purse was made up by George Delany at the Seven Mile-house," reads an article in San Francisco *Chronicle*, dated February 3, 1918. It continues: "…and the purse from the workmen in the Southern Pacific shops; their friendly standing by and sharing with those in distress because they dwelt among them." Even Emma Markt, wife of "Beefsteak Bill," makes a donation—in fact, she does the first round of solicitations, walking around the neighborhood to raise money on the same day of the fire. It's not clear if George Delany was a tenant, an employee, or manager at 7 Mile.

Around this time, the Prohibition Amendment, also known as the 18th Amendment, was passed. The United States had just entered World War I, and President Woodrow Wilson instituted Prohibition to save grain for producing food. Ratified on January

Fireproof

7 Mile House was spared twice from burning. First, it survived the great San Francisco earthquake of 1906 and the major fires that followed—notable if you consider that eighty percent of the city went up in flames.

It escaped destruction again six years after, when a fire razed three structures to the ground—the Red Mill roadhouse, Buffalo Hotel, and a small store used as a saloon—all located nearby, around a mile away from the San Francisco county line. "As a result of relaying water from engine to engine, the Seven Mile House and other property was saved," reads a news article from the San Francisco *Chronicle* on August 21, 1912. "This also stopped the fire from burning the poles of the high tension line, which carries power to the city from the Visitacion station of the San Francisco Gas and Electric Company."

GAMBLING COSTS SALOON PERMITS

"Beefsteak Bill" Markt and Peter Testa Lose Their Licenses.

RESORTS ARE CLOSED UP

Investigation by Supervisors Involves Name of Local Police Sergeant.

After a lengthy hearing the San Mateo Supervisors voted yesterday to cancel the liquor license of William K. Markt, known as "Beefsteak Bill," and Peter Testa, whose saloons just over the San Francisco county line were the scenes of sensational gambling raids several weeks ago.

The hearing was full of interesting disclosures. Not the least startling of these was the testimony of Deputy Sheriff John Shields that the bail money for some of the gamblers arrested during the raid was handed over by a San Francisco police sergeant and that two detectives from the District Attorney's office, who visited Markt's place last Saturday, were assaulted.

According to Shields' testimony, Sergeant de Grancourt of the Potrero station turned over $500 bail money for two of the arrested gamblers. He testified further that he was told that the money was given to De Grancourt by "China Mary," who escaped during the raid, and whom the San Mateo county officers had asked the assistance of the San Francisco police in arresting. W. G. Logan, a San Francisco police officer, who reports to De Grancourt, was the first witness called by J. J. Bullock, former District Attorney of San Mateo county, who acted as Markt's counsel.

DETECTIVES BEATEN UP.

G. W. Gallwey, a private detective, testified that he and C. K. Wood, another operative detailed on the gambling cases, were brutally assaulted by Markt, G. Palecio and "Scotty," Markt's bartender, Saturday afternoon. Wood is at the Lane Hospital in San Francisco and is in danger of losing the sight of one of his eyes. The detectives, Gallwey testified, had been invited by Markt to come into his saloon. He claims that as they mounted the steps they were struck down and badly beaten, Gallwey being attacked by Markt and Wood by the other two men. Gallwey, who received fewer injuries, took Wood to the Potrero Emergency Hospital.

Bullock declared the assault was provoked by Wood and Gallwey attempting to prejudice Markt's wife against him.

GIRL IMPORTANT WITNESS.

One of the principal witnesses against Markt was Mrs. Mary C. Bell, who represented the Juvenile Protective Association of San Francisco. She said that her association had been asked by San Francisco probation officers to investigate young girls dancing in Markt's Real Thing saloon. She also read a letter from Maria

---

Vienna street. NE 25xNW 100. $10.

Bay View Land Company to Eugene Cantet, lots 20 and 21, block 372A, Bay View Tract Subdivision No. 3, grant.

James Henry Gilmore and Jessie P. Gilmore to Michael Benton, lot on S line of Trumbull street, 300 feet E of Craur. E 25x5 100. $500.

Susan Malloy to Bernhard Donnelly, lot on S line of Geary street, 57:6 E of Thirty-seventh avenue, E 25x5 100. $10.

Julia and Andrew Caspar to Vito Mondelli, lot on W line of Wool street, 25 feet S of Eugenia, S 25xW 70. $10.

Palmiro Testa to Niccola Testa, lot 2, block 11, Sunnyvale Homestead Association. $10.

F. W. Nightingill, by F. N. Belgrano et al., to Fugazi Banca Popolare Operia Italiana, lot on S line of Golden Gate avenue, 110 feet E of Buchanan street, W 27:6, S 122:6, E 12:10½, NE 21:9¾, N 120, $1626.50.

Mercantile Trust Company to Winfield S. Davis, lot on N line of Washington street, 103 feet W of Spruce, W 62:6xN 127:8¾. $10.

Winfield and Clara Davis to Bert Schlesinger, lot on N line of Washington street, 103 feet W of Spruce, W 62:6xN 127:8¾. $10.

Bert Schlesinger and wife to Winfield S. Davis, lot on SE corner of Clay and Powell streets, E 59x5 68:9. $10.

Catherine Ivancovich to Samuel S. Parsons, lot on W line of Davis street, 91:5 N of Clay, N 45:10xW 120. $10.

Good Work—Let's Call It A Week and Take Lay Off

Chronicle Home Reconstruction Fund for Stricken Pera Family Totals Over a Thousand—That's Enough!

By HELEN DARE

WE CAN call it a good week's work done and "lay off" now, for The Chronicle's building fund for the Pera family runs over a thousand dollars this morning, and is ample to set them up in a nice new home of their own in comfort—thanks to the unfailing Californian generosity.

Today, under the marshaling of Edward H. Schwerin, the work on the building of the new home begins; the neighbors getting together to prepare the site and saw the lumber for the framework into the required lengths.

Perhaps it's not amiss to confess that it was with fear and trembling the appeal for these poor people here at home was made—after all the drives and demands on purse and sympathy for great and worthy national and international purposes.

Would our home folks be able to come down to earth and consider the modest claims of the poor and obscure, intimate and personal, at their doorstep?

Would we be able to coax even half the generous sum we have totaled from the public that has been called on to give—and has given—so much?

These were the questions that made the undertaking an adventure; and that had to be dared (which isn't a pun) because of the urgency and pitiful need.

ANSWER IS SPLENDID

How they have been answered by ready, cordial, tender sympathy and generosity is evident in the result The Chronicle can give you this morning.

It is splendid proof of the community feeling that when there is need of reconstruction work here at home our home folks are right on the job to do it.

Everything that kindness and friendliness could think of has been showered on the Pera family to mitigate their misfortune—even a job for Louis Pera; for Corporal Brown of the Bay View police telephoned in yesterday that he had work for him at the Southern Pacific shops newly established in Visitacion valley; so now, Louis will not have to walk four miles from his work (as he's been doing) to save carfare to apply to the H. C. L.

Mrs. A. J. Bartley added to our collection a pair of fine, warm, double blankets; Edmond Jones of the Hotel Majestic has kitchen utensils, dishes and tableware for them; Tony Canepa "two nice complete beds," and—

Listen to this:

There's even a doll for little seven-year-old Julia. She came in a big box, "For Little Miss Pera," from a blessed little girl at Fort Scott, a beauty of

the people in the valley, and by 'the evening of the day on which they were burned out we had $26.25 for them. When I offered it to Pera he didn't want to take it; he said he had $5 of his own, and I had to squeeze it into his hand. Then T. E. Schwerin gave them $25 more, and the Coroner raised a purse for them at the inquest, and so the funeral of the two children was provided for.

CHRONICLE COMES TO AID

"Of course, we couldn't stop there, for we knew they had nothing to begin with again; as Mrs. Markt, Mrs. Stroup and I came up with a little starter from the neighborhood, never thinking then that The Chronicle gave—and in that way we got together $74 more"—which was the $74 he brought in and added to the Chronicle building fund.

It was thus that—while the ashes of the destroyed house were still hot, the smoke still drifting above them, and the charred bodies of the little children awaiting burial—the neighborliness of Visitacion Valley was proved with the common sentiment that:

"It was the least we could do for them."

Came with this also the offer of their help—to work on Sundays and in such free time as they could give—in building the new home.

To this was added, in neighborliness, the purse made up by George Delany at the Seven-mile House, and the purse from the workmen in the Southern Pacific shops; their friendly standing by and sharing with those in distress because they dwelt among them.

It's an impulse, and a practice, as old as human groupings, no doubt; and it is good to find evidence that it persists.

BABY HEARTS RESPOND

In all the inpouring of gifts from the "outsiders" that proved the answering humanity to human need, none were more tender and generous, more inspiring than the little gifts; that "orphan's mite" of 20 cents, the bright little dime from a child, "for the Pera family"; the 22 pennies from the juvenile bank, the dollar that was four little "Samaritans" movie money, and the dime that came with this letter telling The Chronicle editor:

"I am a little girl without a papa and my mamma has to work, but I want you to use this 10 cents to buy nails. It is all I can give, but it will help."

"From a little girl named Mercedes."

"P. S.—May God bless these poor people, like he has my mamma, sister Ina and myself."

With sidelights like these this old

---

to 150
to 350

eceipts, higher; : light, $7.20@ .to 75c. . $8.25. higher; : cows @19.75. higher; 5@7.75;

S. 1270 sacks of

S. Out-3 cents hurrahs. kip, 5 urths of t hides, , and 1 identical. ers, 16

Four year formed tha her husband O'Conery, re ment and the child.

O'Conery Mrs. Biers, went to M that O'Cone fled. She s and finally ing her st said:

"For man nearly mad my daughter presentimer I find some be forced Lake and looking for O'Conery v neapolis, bi and for ten ing of him

---

Palmiro, having taken the Americanized nickname of "Peter," had his liquor license revoked when 7 Mile became one of the targets (the other being Real Thing Saloon) of anti-gambling raids in 1914. Three years after, he transferred his Sunnyvale Homestead property to his wife and bade the saloon scene goodbye, opening a cigar shop in Santa Rosa. 7 Mile resurfaces in the news again in 1918, when a certain George Delany, resident of 7 Mille, makes a charitable donation to a family who had lost their home to a fire.

4

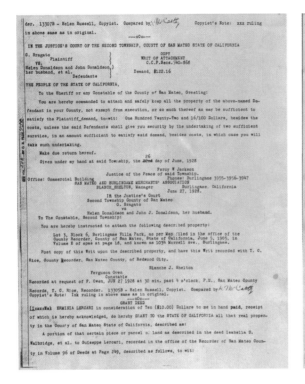
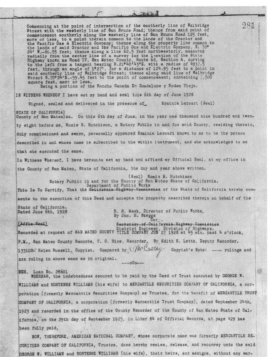

In 1928, Giuseppi Lercari granted the Bayshore-Geneva corner lot to his wife, Erminia. I find it amusing that the legal preamble of the parcel obtained has not changed since; every period and comma and archaic turn of phrase remains as it was when it was written in 1928.

29, 1919, it went into effect in 1920. Also known as the Volstead Act after the chairman of the House Judiciary Committee Representative Andrew Volstead of Mississippi, Prohibition was the "legal prevention of the manufacture, sale, and transportation of alcoholic beverages in the United States from 1920 to 1933 under the terms of the 18th Amendment."

But people liked their poison, and were willing to risk buying and drinking illegally produced spirits just to get their fix. Bootlegging and speakeasies became lucrative businesses, especially

Leslie O. Jacobs, Daniel E. Koshland, Sid Levy, D. Michael, M. M. Robinson and S. L. Samter.

200-Gallon Still Seized
Three Suspects Jailed

Three men were arrested in a raid of Federal prohibition agents at 125 Ashton avenue early yesterday. Agents assert they seized a 200-gallon whisky still and a truck loaded with 220 gallons of alcohol. Those in custody are Pedro Pessaglio, Alfred Ciargello and Sebastiano Nieri. Agents arrested Fred Freitas on Webster street charged with the transportation of a small quantity of beer, and John Reide in a raid at 114 Embarcadero.

MISSING WIFE SOUGHT

Expressing the belief that his

Sebastiano Nieri and Lawrence Frugoli were the third and fourth owners of 7 Mile; the first to both own the establishment and the land, which they had appraised in 1941. (Above left) Nieri seems to have had a wild streak, as his name comes up in the papers in 1932 as being involved in the possession of a whisky still and the transport of alcohol during Prohibition. (Above right) Southern Pacific Bayshore machine shop workers in 1935, taken across the street from 7 Mile House. We can only imagine how many of these young men walked into 7 Mile and had a drink or two after a hard days' work. (SanFranciscoTrains.org; Walter Boland collection, copyright 2014)

among those who had the resources and the chutzpah—mostly organized gangs who meted out violence against each other in turf wars. By 1932, however, and as the country entered deeper into the Great Depression, legalizing the selling and manufacturing of liquor—and thereby creating

Sanfranciscotrains.org
Copyright W.Boland 2014

more jobs and revenue—began to sound like a good idea. This was part of Franklin D. Roosevelt's platform when he ran for president that year; he won, and by December 1933, the last vote for ratification of the 21st Amendment to repeal the 18th was submitted.

None of the documents and newspaper articles we found explicitly said who owned 7 Mile during the Prohibition, but if we were to assume based on the dates of the real estate appraisal report and news clippings at the time, we can come up with two names: Lawrence Frugoli and Sebastiano Nieri. They were the first individuals who both owned the land, as well as the establishment. The property was first appraised in May 1941, and we can deduce that they bought it from Erminia Lercari. Erminia was Giuseppi Lercari's wife, to whom he granted the land in June 1928.

Sebastiano and Lawrence appeared to be enterprising in all areas, but weren't sticklers for

Bayshore City:
A GAMBLERS' HAVEN

Books from the early 20th century wax poetic about the richness of San Mateo County's land—ie., "this land possesses great fertility and produces fine crops of cereals...many small tracts and little valleys in the mountains are carefully tilled, yielding abundant harvests of grain, and producing luxuriant growths of fruits and vegetables."

Despite its fertile beauty, San Mateo was thinly populated. It was referred to as "the country" by San Franciscans, a place where crimes could be committed unhindered. Mitchell P. Postel, in *San Mateo County, A Sesquicentennial History*, writes that: "If you couldn't get away with it in San Francisco (and that was saying a lot), then you could simply cross the county line, where law enforcement was weak, when available, and not present most of the time."

When boxing, or prizefighting, was made illegal in San Francisco, the fights were moved to San Mateo. During Prohibition, bootleggers would sneak down along the bay; almost every town had their own producers of moonshine. Things didn't change much after the repeal of Prohibition. By the 1930s to 1940s, illegal gambling had become the domain of gangsters, and they ran everything from dog racing to gambling houses. It didn't help that the public had taken on a cynical view towards law enforcement and political reform. Most of the gangsters were much more powerful, with connections in the East. It was a glorious time for bookies, who brokered bets in the illegal races. They raked it in.

In 1932, "Bayshore City"—which was actually just a budding town near the Cow Palace—was incorporated. This was established "for no other purpose than to operate a dog track and, not so secretly, gambling houses," writes Postel. It even had its own city council and chief of police. It even had investors— Chinese gamblers got wind of Bayshore City, and managed to get concessions for their Bayshore City Club and the Oriental Gambling Emporium, the biggest in the county at that time.

But all good things come to an end. Under pressure from the community, the State Crime Commission closed down the Emporium. When dog racing was outlawed in 1939, Bayshore City was likewise disincorporated. It annexed to Daly City in 1963.

A Google Earth screenshot of how our location looked like in 1938. Around the area of the Cow Palace was the site of Bayshore City.

DOG TRACK

COW PALACE

P.G.+E. YARD

7 MILE

S.P. RAILYARD

768 Woodside road: C. Silvani, Charlie's Place, 728 Woodside road; Carlo Ferrando, Carlo's Place, 1705 El Camino Real; Frank M. Garcia, Frank's Place, 2231 El Camino Real; Joseph Temperani, 2303 El Camino Real; P. A. Caruso and C. Nelson, 2030 Club, 2030 Broadway; and G. Pierazzi, L. W. Foss and L. McNichol, The Deacon, 1328 El Camino Real.

South San Francisco: Elizabeth Firenze, S. F. club, 1001 Bayshore highway; Angelo Columbo and Joe Mainini, Linden hotel, 208 Linden avenue; V. Massetti and John Marchi, Town House, 115 Grand avenue; Angelo and Earnest Genovesi, Bombay club, 206 Grand avenue; Eugene Milani, Milani's tavern, 935 Bayshore boulevard; P. Questoni and B. F. Foppiano, Babe's cafe, 201 Grand avenue; Luisa Cattaneo, the Topper, 249 Grand avenue; Roger De Luca; John Fanucchi, Airport tavern, 227 Grand avenue; Assunta Barsuglia, 222 Lux avenue; Silvio Dubiosi, 207 Grand avenue; Eva Belli, Belli's Place, 75 First street; Andrew Colombani, Jim Laricchia, and Paul Fleming, Orange tavern, 599 Orange avenue; Simone and Rose Parolini, the Derby, 241 Grand avenue; Herman Gambero, Swing club, 751 Bayshore boulevard; Alphonse Ferrari, 100-102 Grand avenue; Nellie Agresti, Nellie's Place, 63 El Camino Real; George Molinari, Molinari's, 301-303 Grand avenue; and George H. Wallace Sr., Blue Ribbon tavern, 257 Grand avenue.

Daly City: Ruby Koop, Witt's End, 6055 Mission street; Andrea O. Sardi, The Central Club, 6282 Mission street; F. C. Britton, R. B. and V. L. Dodson, Tiny's, 6045 Mission street; John M. Griffith and D. H. Ely, Jolly Trio, 6290 Mission street; Sam J. and Anthony Parmisano, Veterans' Inn, 6025 Mission street; Marie Sullivan, Mission Belle Chateau, 6143 Mission street; Thomas J. and Louise Plant, Jack's Inn, 640Y Mission street; Luella and Ec---ard Holmgren, Goodfellows, 7123 Mission street; Beula J. Berkhout, Hill Crest, 22 Hillcrest drive: and George Kirchhubel, Kirchhubel's, 6296 Mission street.

Millbrae: John Comolo, John's, El Camino Real and Silva street; Adelina Sartori, Richie's Inn, El Camino Real, Louisa Lichezzola, Sunny Side Inn, El Camino Real; George D'Olivo, Highlands Inn, 333 El Camino Real, and Joseph Bonzani, Tip Top Inn, 210 El Camino Real.

Brisbane: John DeMarco, 23 Club, 23 Visitacion avenue; Giovanni Bernardini, Dick's Tower, 2 Visitacion avenue; Bert Mazzuco, Tourist Cafe, San Bruno road and Visitacion avenue, and Joe and Charles Mozzetti, Mozzetti Brothers, Bayshore highway.

Colma: Daniel J. Silvestri, Bocchi Ball, Rainier street; Pera Giulio and Irma Togholi, Stumble Inn, Hillside and Castle streets; Pasquale Ramacciotti, Hillside Club, Hillside boulevard, and Frank Molloy, Molloy's Springs, Colma.

Bayshore City: Charles Goletti, Charlie's, 2614 Geneva avenue; S. Nieri and L. Fruguli, 7 Mile House, Bayshore and Geneva avenue, and Harry and Robert Flynn, Harry's Geneva Club, 2601 Geneva avenue.

San Carlos: Natalino Ciampi, Hidden Valley Inn, 21 Wellington drive; Sydney Levin, The Carlos Club, 612 El Camino Real, and T. W. Carpenter, M. P. Bates and John E. Lewis, The Stork Club, 1240 El Camino Real.

San Bruno: Arthur E. Annis and F. J. Mason, 458 Club, 458 San Mateo avenue; Tyler C. Wilson, Legion Club, 757 San Mateo avenue, and Frank Stumpf and A. J. Ballati, Walter's Place, 418 San Mateo avenue.

Lomita Park: C. P. Hart, Dog House, Santo Domingo and

77 S.M. Bars Accused of Serving Drink, No Food

County Joins in Bid for S.F. State College

PUBLIC APPEAL SEEN TO SAVE RUTANO BILL

Penalties Seen If They Fail to Begin Reilly

PRESIDENT, TAFT BOTH ON RADIO TONIGHT TO

Man Shot In Family Quarrel

An Ingleside mechanic was shot in the leg and his wife was fired upon when she ran for help from their home, 219 Broad street, following an argument with two guests last night.

Leonard Stuehler, 29, was treated at Alemany Emergency Hospital for the bullet wound. Bertram Kelly, 29, 275 Orizabo street, was treated for a scalp wound suffered when he was hit with the revolver butt.

Chester Lindsey, 30, was held by police for investigation.

Officer Thomas Dempsey said Kelly and Lindsey, distant relatives of Stuehler, had called at Stuehler's home at 11:30 p. m., becoming abusive during an argument.

Stuehler threatened to get his revolver from a desk, police said. Kelly reached the weapon first but it was retrieved by Stuehler who allegedly struck Kelly over the head with it. Kelly then seized the gun and shot Stuehler.

Lindsey then got hold of the weapon and assertedly fired three times without effect at Mrs. Stuehler when she ran to a neighbor's to summon police.

In the meantime, Stuehler went to his car and got another pistol. He was returning to the scene when Officers Ed Cantwell and Thomas Ryan arrived and disarmed him.

Lindsey and Kelly are brothers-in-law residing at the same address. They are warehousemen.

7 Mile House, along with seventy-six other bars in San Mateo County, was charged for not serving food in 1947. Town House of South San Francisco was also charged. This is worth a mention since Town House owner John Marchi would later partner with Camille and Lenny Stuehler as co-proprietor of 7 Mile House.

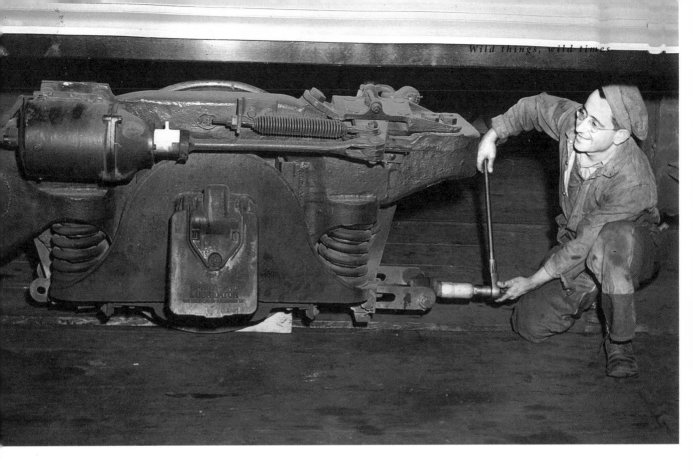

Southern Pacific railyard worker Joseph I. Bosso, father of 7 Mile House customers Joe and Steve Bosso, in the 1940s. Joseph worked there from 1941 to 1984.

properly running a bar and following the rules. In 1932, Sebastiano Nieri, along with two other men, was arrested for transporting whisky. A San Francisco *Chronicle* story printed on January 27, 1932 says that Nieri was caught with a 200-gallon whisky still, and 220 gallons of alcohol in his truck. In 1947, 7 Mile House was charged with something that would be impossible today: it was among the seventy-seven bars in San Mateo County who were charged with not serving food. "The specific violation laid to the bars covers failure to serve foods at all hours when they are open and serving liquor," reads an article in the San Mateo *Times* on June 20, 1947. "It is covered by Section 22 of Article XX of the State Constitution and Section 53 of the Alcohol Beverage Control Act." Our *adobo* and 7 Mile Burger fans would freak if this happened today.

Then, in July 1948, four slot machines were found in 7 Mile House. The four machines—"one large and modern console type—and three one-armed bandit type"—were not in operation. But they were confiscated by the police and an invitation was put out to the public for claimants. While Sebastian and Lawrence were denying ownership of these machines, not too far away, in Ingleside, a man was recovering from a gunshot to the leg. He had been in a fight around the time the four slot machines were found; an argument with a distant relative had gone south, and both he and his wife were fired upon. The man was Leonard "Lenny" Stuehler, and the wife, Camille Faccini Stuehler. If it weren't for Camille's quick thinking—she had run for help just before things got really ugly—Lenny might not have made it out of the fight alive. But he did. He and Camille would be the next owners of the 7 Mile House, imbuing it over the next five decades with equal amounts of infamy, warmth, and oddball appeal.

THE PUGILIST PAINTER

Tommy Egan was a boxer who frequented 7 Mile House. He was also a painter, whose talents were put to good use in his favorite dive. During Camille's time, he was commissioned to do two paintings to cover the mirrors behind the bar. Apparently, customers would catch other men looking at their girlfriends or dates in the mirrors, and this would lead to many a fistfight.

(Above) An autographed photo of Tommy still hangs on the wall in 7 Mile House today. (Left) A full shot of the bar in the 1990s. You'll see the paintings on either end of the bar. (Below) A closer look at the painting can be seen behind Al Flynn. This was taken during his last day as owner of the restaurant.

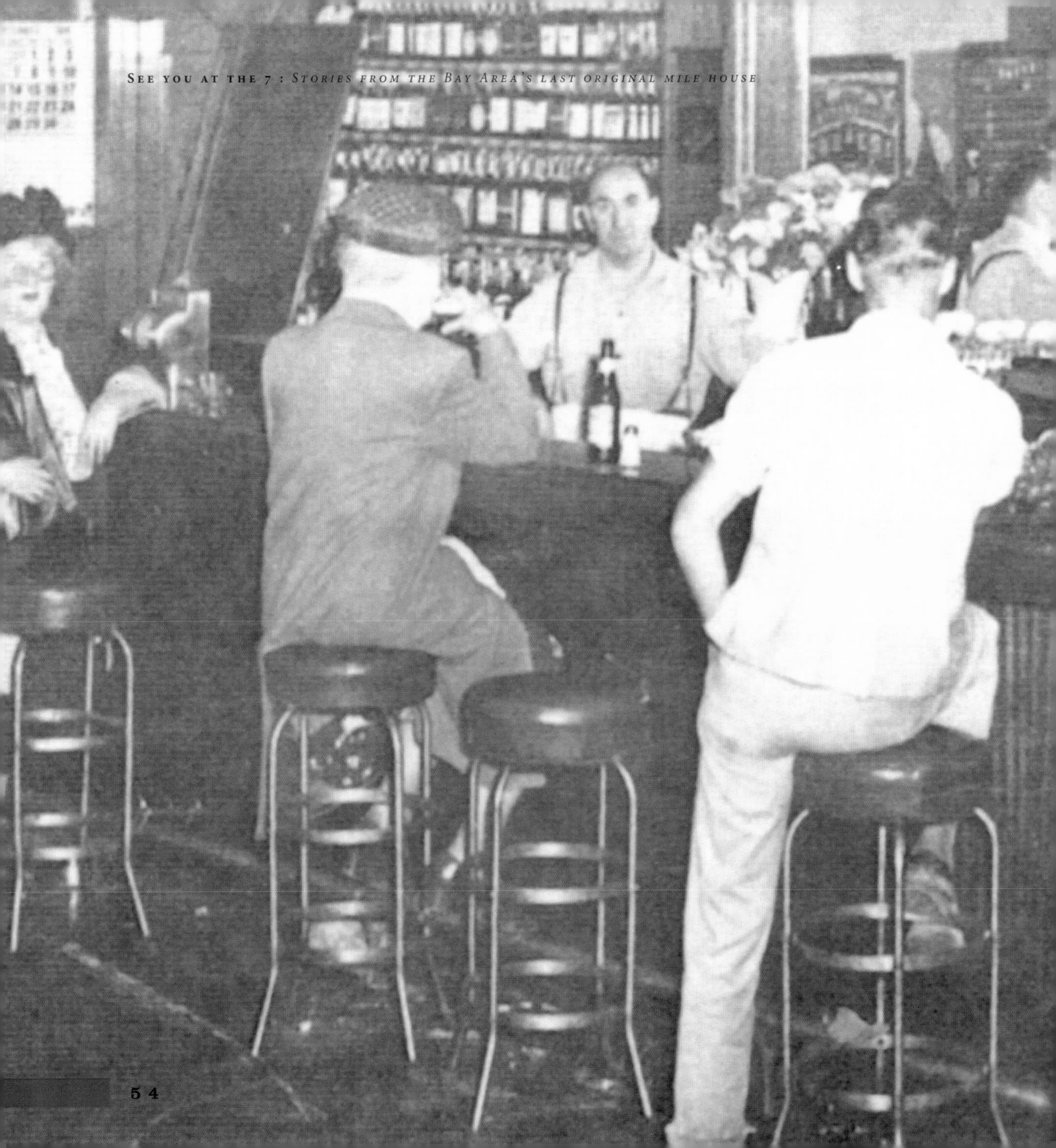

NONE OF THE **DOCUMENTS FOUND EXPLICITLY** SAID WHO OWNED **7 MILE** DURING THE **PROHIBITION**, BUT IF WE WERE TO ASSUME **BASED ON DATES** OF THE REAL ESTATE APPRAISAL REPORT AND NEWS AT THE TIME, WE CAN COME UP WITH TWO NAMES: **LAWRENCE FRUGOLI** AND **SEBASTIAN NIERI.**

An uncaptioned photo of a bar scene from the 7 Mile House in the 1940s.

3

LOVE

and

EQUALITY

at

7 MILE

GETTING TO KNOW LENNY STUEHLER, DEALING WITH THE RACE ISSUE IN THE 1950s, AND FINDING LOVE IN THE HAPPIEST PLACE THIS SIDE OF NOWHERE (1953-1965)

I came to the U.S., ostensibly, because of love. Isn't that the reason most twenty-two-year-olds have when choosing to uproot from their home, leaving everything they know behind?

He was a nice boy from the mid-West—blond, outdoorsy, big smile… stereotypical American kid. He came to the Philippines to work at a theme park, and I met him at one of our gigs (I played the drums with an all-girl band in the Nineties), and, as young people are wont to do, we did impulsive, irresponsible things in the name of fun: learned to scuba dive in a day, under a dubious dive instructor; ran in our bathrobes in the chilly hills of Tagaytay; smashed in my car window when we forgot the keys on an escape to Subic Bay. The plan was to come from my native Philippines on a tourist visa, get a student visa, and settle in as one of the countless immigrants who would embrace the U.S. as their home. Just weeks before I was to fly out, however, he sent me a very heartfelt message: "You're too ambitious for me," he said. He was afraid that if we ended up together, he would hold me back. While I wanted to soar, he was content in his own stratosphere. He would be the sandbag to my air balloon, he said. Or something like that.

It was a smooth breakup—if he was lying, how do you argue with something so seemingly

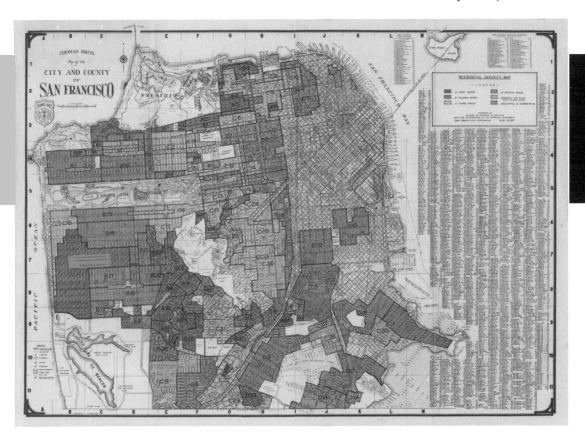

I was warned I might experience racism when I came to the U.S., but thankfully, I never felt it. It galls me to think the concept exists. Above is a color-coded zoning map; these were distributed in the 1920s to 1930s by federal housing agencies so banks could identify places where they could back loans. Filmore, a predominantly black and Asian neighborhood, was outlined in red—a "take caution" zone. (Previous page) 7 Mile House in 1949. The windmill is gone; in its place is a water tank.

sincere and, well, true? But if he was being truthful, then that breakup was probably one of the most selfless things anyone has done for me.

I forged ahead with the plan anyway, sans boyfriend. I came to San Francisco, looked for a school where I could get a master's degree, and began my integration into American society. I've heard warnings about how hard a time I might have, with Filipinos being treated differently, or how I might never feel like I belonged. But from the moment I set foot here till this day, I have never experienced discrimination—at least not personally. Or maybe I'm just blind, or refuse to see that a human being would be so cruel as to consider another human being inferior, just because of the color of their skin.

But while San Francisco—and California, for that matter—is a largely diverse and tolerant city, there are pockets of racism throughout its history. There was the Chinese Exclusion Act of 1882, the creation of the Federal Housing Administration in 1934, and San Francisco's post-war Redevelopment Authority, which eased out and restricted many rights from people due to their skin color. In neighborhoods already made up of minorities, there was still racism—Italians against the Irish, Germans against Italians. A sad reality that even the brightest Pollyanas cannot erase or deny.

One beautiful thing I've always observed, and what was reaffirmed while making this book, was that 7 Mile House has never been a place where discrimination happens. There may be hatred festering outside, but once you step inside those two doors, all resentment and animosity vanish. "Never!," everyone I talked to declared, when asked if they ever felt uncomfortable or out of place at 7 Mile. "Never!"

This was reassuring, considering the forces that were simmering throughout the United States in the 1950s: a resurgence

Camille left behind a date stamp from the 1940s,
old business cards, and a nifty calendar-paper clip holder.

MAYBE I'M JUST BLIND, OR REFUSE TO SEE THAT A HUMAN BEING WOULD BE SO CRUEL AS TO CONSIDER ANOTHER HUMAN BEING INFERIOR, JUST BECAUSE OF THE COLOR OF THEIR SKIN.

Bar Owner Fined For Selling To Minors

SOUTH SAN FRANCISCO, Sept. 20.—John Marchi, 46, of 818 Grand avenue, owner of a local tavern, was yesterday fined $100 in police court when he pleaded guilty to charges of selling liquor to minors. The two minors, Floyd and Lloyd Holson twin brothers, 18, of 404 Victory avenue, were sentenced by Judge S. K. Robbins to serve 30 days in the county jail and the jail sentence was suspended on the condition that they leave the state.

Wins $10,000 For Beating In Bar Brawl

REDWOOD CITY —. A superior court jury here has awarded $10,000 damages to a South San Francisco meat packer who was beaten in a bar in 1957.

Winner of the award is Roy M. Crum. Defendants in the case were John Marchi and Georgia A. Lombardi, owners of the Ladle club on Airport boulevard in South Francisco, and Edmunde O. Sanford, a San Mateo steel worker.

Crum said he and Sanford were patrons in the bar on November 13, 1957, when Sanford assaulted him and knocked him to the floor. He alleged that the owners failed to protect him from Sanford and failed to call police after the attack.

Crum said he left the bar and was walking up the concrete stairs of his home at 842 Commercial avenue when he collapsed and fell, suffering a skull fracture, loss of speech, partial paralysis and other injuries.

The jury brought in the $10,000 verdict following a three-day trial in the courtroom of Superior Judge Edmund Scott.

If John Marchi's business partnership with Camille and Lenny had lasted longer, they would have had enough antics between them to fill an entire long-running television series: Marchi was fined in 1947 for selling liquor to minors, and in 1960, he and his Ladle Club partner lost a case against a man who had been beaten up in their bar.

of the Ku Klux Clan along with the Civil Rights movement, and residual sentiment against Mexicans for overpowering Americans at The Alamo, and towards the Japanese for World War II.

But it was also the era of the television set, when Americans enjoyed classics like "I Love Lucy," "The Ed Sullivan Show," or "Gunsmoke." It was the era of Beat poets and Audrey Hepburn, Fats Domino and Frank Sinatra, B.B. King and The Platters. Though history books tell us that the general atmosphere of the 1950s bore a sense of sexual and social conservatism, the era's biggest icons represented anything but that: Elvis, Marilyn, and James.

This was the decade wherein 7 Mile House's most colorful owners to date, purchased the place: Leonard (or Lenny) and Camille Stuehler, then both in their mid-thirties, and who figured a lot in the local papers when it came to accidents and fracas. They were joined by a certain George Roberts, according to a couple of newspaper articles, and whom Rick Stuehler, Lenny's nephew, remembers as "Robert." At one point, the Stuehler couple also partnered with John Marchi, who owned The Ladle Club and Town House taverns in South San Francisco.

The property on which 7 Mile House stood was reappraised for Lawrence Frugoli in June 1953, and Camille and Lenny appeared in the San Mateo *Times* in November of the same year for being in a major accident in Redwood City. They were referred to in the article as being owners of 7 Mile House, so we assume that they leased the bar from Frugoli and his partner Sebastiano Nieri a little after the reappraisal. Less than a year after, the 7 Mile House was burglarized at six in the morning—it was hit more than once during Camille's tenure as the owner—with the robbers beating up the janitor and taking off with $2,300 from the safe. The same safe—which is at least sixty years old—is still there, actually. And no, I don't keep anything in it anymore. (Incidentally, there is also a floor safe that no one—not in Al Flynn's time, not in Camille or Lenny's time—remembers ever having been opened.)

From 1953 to 2004, the Stuehler name was synonymous with the 7 Mile House. They stuck with it through thick and thin, through burglaries, illnesses, indictments, the evolution of bartenders and regulars. What was it about Lenny and Camille that made them so headstrong and foolhardy? What was it about them that made them able to build up a glorious space, a safe space, such as 7 Mile? What was it about 7 Mile House that made the regulars—the oldest regulars today that we could get ahold of—stay, and visit time and time again? I can only surmise. To get the real undiluted stories, I had to go to the sources themselves—whoever was available and willing to talk. And when we could, we always talked onsite at 7 Mile, their happy place of yesteryear.

Remembering

UNCLE
LENNY

As told by

RICK STUEHLER

ncle Lenny was the only person in San Mateo County who had ever been arrested for D.U.I on a horse.

He had some horses on Skyline Boulevard, and he went up one day and had been drinking way too much. He lost his keys and couldn't get his truck going, so he rode his horse back to Millbrae, and the police later arrested him for drunkenness. He was pretty famous for that. Al Flynn bailed him out.

Our family was small. We didn't have a lot of relatives and didn't see my Uncle Lenny that often. He'd come up, stay for an hour or two, and then leave. We always loved to see Uncle Len. My dad and Uncle Lenny couldn't be more different, and my dad always wished that Uncle Len would take care of himself better.

My grandfather, August Christian Berthold Stuehler, and grandmother, Francizka Wimmer, came from Germany and Austria through Ellis Island in 1905. There was no financial opportunity for anyone in Europe at that time; the way the *kaisers* were running things then was that if you were a blacksmith, you would be a blacksmith all your life. There was no educational or upward mobility for anyone. I think my grandmother was sixteen years old and my grandfather, much older. I think they got married in the New York-New Jersey area. What family we had stayed in the East Coast. Few family came to the west.

My grandfather worked as a *maitre d'* in some of the nicer restaurants and hotels downtown, and my grandmother worked

On June 25, 1956, the San Mateo Times *report that a man had been riding his horse drunk. Said man was Lenny Stuehler.*

Hi-Yo Silver! At 4 o'Clock In the Morning

(Times Peninsula News Service)

MILLBRAE, June 25 — Police here were startled early yesterday morning (about 4 a.m.), to receive a radio call that a drunk was just seen riding a white horse down Bayview avenue.

Rushing to the area, Officers William Urbanski and Ozzie Splivalo reported they found Leonard Stuehler, 35, a bar owner of 539 Bayview avenue, Millbrae, hiding behind a high hedge in front of his home, holding the white horse.

Stuehler explained that he had driven to the Skyline boulevard in his pickup truck to treat a second horse owned by him for a lame foot. But then, he said, he lost the keys to the truck and decided to go horseback to his home.

Although Stuehler allegedly swung at Splivalo when he attempted to place him in the police car, Urbanski reported he was unable to help because he was holding the horse. When Mrs. Stuehler came from the house and took over the custody of the horse, the two officers arrested Stuehler on a charge of drunkenness. He was taken to the Hillsborough city jail and later released on $50 bail.

Before owning 7 Mile House, Lenny ran an ambulance service. Here he is with one of his vehicles circa 1950. It was a down and dirty business, one that matched Lenny's streetsmarts and guts perfectly. (Previous page) Leonard Stuehler looking dapper in the 1950s.

in a bakery. They had two sons—my dad, Berthold, and my uncle, born in 1916 and 1919—born in Daly City in the Outer Mission off of Crocker Avenue and Peoria Street. My dad went on to medical school and became a general practitioner and practiced out of St. Luke's hospital. I don't know if my uncle had an education beyond high school.

The only job I know that he held before he bought the 7 Mile House was that he owned an ambulance service. Back in those days, there were no emergency medical technicians and paramedics. If you were in an accident or injured or sick, they'd put you in a gurney and haul you

7 Mile was a working man's bar, says Rick. Men with unusual shifts from the railyard and factories in the area would drop in any time of day. They paid for their drinks with their hard-earned money. (Left) The Southern Pacific railyard boiler shop crew, likely during a Christmas party. Employees from Southern Pacific used to come into 7 Mile House for steaks. (Below) A sample of what their paychecks looked like then.

Eugene O'Connor Collection   Bayshore Boiler Shop, San Francisco, CA.   sanfranciscotrains.org 2011

2-46 - 400M

SOUTHERN PACIFIC COMPANY
STATEMENT OF EMPLOYE'S EARNINGS AND DEDUCTIONS

32520   S-9897

EARNINGS		
Total earnings including adjustments	163	02
DEDUCTIONS		
Int. Rev. Code Ch. 9B ("Retirement")	5	71
Federal Withholding Tax	24	50
Group Life Insurance		
Hospital Department	2	75
U. S. Saving Bonds	37	50
Local Watch Inspector		
Local Eating Houses		
Miscellaneous - (Symbol) *		
"		
"		
"		
Time Voucher Issued		

*See reverse side for explanation of symbols

FIRST PERIOD   92.56

65   JULY   1946   61
E-1
1.235   ȾȾȾȾȾ ȾȾ   65
FRED BOLAND

IMPORTANT

Your earnings and Federal Withholding Tax shown hereon will be reported to Federal and State Agencies for tax purposes. You should retain this statement for your record. It is important that Social Security Account number and name as carried on pay roll agree with that shown on your Social Security identification card. In event of discrepancy in either number or name please notify your supervisor immediately.

(SanFranciscoTrains.org; Eugene O'Connor collection, copyright 2011 (top) and Walter Boland collection, copyright 2014 (above)

I GUESS MY DAD FELT BAD FOR MY UNCLE BECAUSE HE NEVER HAD CHILDREN, SO HE "LOANED" ME TO MY UNCLE LENNY.

to the closest hospital. They used a regular broadcast radio, and the police would announce like in the old movies where they'd go "calling all cars, calling all cars" — that's how it was then, they didn't have two-way radio. So all of the people, like the tow truck, ambulance, they all listened to that same frequency. The first guy who got there got the job. It was a kind of a down and dirty business. Lenny did that for several years.

I was six or seven years old when my uncle bought the bar, in 1953. Lenny and Camille had a partner named Robert. That left side of 7 Mile that has a concrete wall used to be a cyclone fence about four feet tall. You could look through it, and you could see "Lenny, Camille, and Robert" painted with white letters. It's probably still on there. I never met Robert because he was out of the scene, and then one day he was gone and Lenny and Cam were the sole owners.

My first time in the 7 Mile was maybe when I was ten years old. My dad's office being in the Outer Mission, we used to have lunch frequently in the bowling alley up on Geneva, near Cow Palace. My grandmother was still alive in the same house on Peoria St. Uncle Len and my dad took care of her till she passed away. When she did, they sold the house and my uncle spent his adult life in Millbrae.

7 Mile's business back then was usually in the afternoon or early evenings. They didn't have a dinner trade; they tried lunch but it didn't work out. Some families went, but mainly to hang out. There was nothing to eat, but Len had plenty of snacks. In some cases, some people were there with their grandparents.

It was mainly a working man's bar with regulars who came from Crown, Cork, and Seal — that used to be a little bit north where Geneva came in to Old Bayshore. They made things like bottling equipment for Coca-Cola. Another was Schlage Lock, that made door locks. Then across the street was the Southern Pacific railyard. They used to get a lot of the railroad guys with unusual shifts. They could be there any time of the day, morning, afternoon, late at night. Most of the fellows I remember

OTHER GUYS WOULD COME IN AND THEY WOULD **WANT TO BUY A DRINK** AND THEY DIDN'T HAVE ANY MONEY. **AND MY UNCLE,** HE WAS LIKE A PAWNSHOP. HE WOULD TRADE **RADIOS, TVs, CARS** FOR DRINKS.

were in coveralls covered in grease and dirt. I would say several hundred men worked in that yard back then. There were always guys going to that corner of Geneva and coming back.

I found this all out when I was around thirteen. I guess my dad felt bad for my uncle because he never had children, so he "loaned" me to my Uncle Lenny. My dad would drop me off at Millbrae, go off to his office. I'd spend the day with my uncle, and he'd take me home. Sometimes, I'd go up on a Saturday morning, do cleaning, take boxes of booze from a room at the back of the bar, unpack them, and put them on the shelves.

When you'd walk in the front door, there was a bar straight ahead. On the right and left side, there were booths against the wall, and two or three tables in the middle. I'm not sure how many seats there were but I'll say in the neighborhood of twenty. When I went in there most of the guys were belly up to the bar. The bar was always full. Then there was a door to the left that went out to the storage area.

My uncle would pour me a Coke, shoot the breeze with the customers, talk to whoever—the bartender or Camille, on what they needed or whatever. And someone would come up to me, ask how's school, how's everything. I used to watch these guys; it was funny because someone was always playing Liar's Dice, and they'd pass the cup around—"who's going to pay for this round?" —and most of these guys could hoist their drinks, and they would win, win, and suddenly this guy's got these drinks in front of him, and he's drinking three drinks simultaneously.

I used to wonder if these regulars had jobs—every time I went there, they were the same guys.

Other guys would come in and they would want to buy a drink and they didn't have any money. And my uncle, he was like a pawnshop. He would trade radios, TVs, cars, for drinks. Imagine driving in there and giving away your car. So he would collect quite a few cars from guys

Rick Stuehler at fifteen years old. For his sixteenth birthday, Uncle Lenny promised him a
De Soto, which a customer had pawned at the bar. But before Rick reached sixteen, Lenny had
crashed the car into a telephone pole. However, his uncle kept true to his promise and, together, Rick
and Lenny fixed up the De Soto. Unfortunately, the brakes overheated and it never ran again.

who owed him money. He was working the late shift at one point, and he was drinking as much or more than his patrons were. On more than one occasion, he crashed into something with one car, and there were always three or four extra cars parked out front. When one got badly wrecked, he just picked up another one.

One day, a guy came in who had a beautiful 1949 De Soto. Somehow, the guy needed money, my uncle handed him the money, and the car ended up in his house.

I was over at his house one day working, and he said to me, "this car is for you when you turn sixteen." It was a beautiful car. Perfect. I could not have been more excited. Well, within six months, Uncle Len ran into a telephone pole with that car. There was a big V-shaped dent that went right into the radiator and everything.

But then later when I was sixteen, he told me, we're going to fix that De Soto. We went down to the auto supply store and we got stuff to solder up the radiator that had been pushed into the fan. We spent all fixing it, and my uncle hands me the keys and says, "here, take it out for the spin." I didn't have a driver's license then but I knew how to drive. I took it up to Larksberg Drive up to Skyline Boulevard and as I got towards the top of the hill, the radiator exploded. Steam and hot water everywhere. So I turned around—Larksberg is a very steep hill—and started down the hill. I had no engine. As I'm getting down to the bottom of the hill, the brakes overheated and I couldn't stop the car. At the bottom of the curve, around Bayview, where he lived, there's a four-way stop sign, and I couldn't get the car down to less than thirty-five miles an hour. I sailed right through the stop sign, up to the hill on the other side, down that hill, and finally, I got to a level spot behind his house on the street over. The brakes were on fire, and I walked home. He came over with me, and we got the car started. We parked it in front of his house, and it never ran again. That was the end of my De Soto. It was the most disappointing day in my young life.

It was around 1960 when my uncle tried to open the restaurant section again. When he did, I would go up there to have lunch. But my uncle and aunt weren't big on doing a lot of cooking. Maybe he was hoping lunch could make up for lost income from losing concession for some claw machines. But it didn't cut it.

Back in the Fifties, they used to have these machines in the bars—you put in a quarter, this big claw with a chain would come down, and you'd pick up a toy or a present and drop it in the chute. My uncle owned about fifty of these claw machines, and he had them in bars all over San Francisco. This was his side business. By the late 1950s, the State of California classified this as a gambling device and it was outlawed for the time being. My uncle's basement in Millbrae was full of these machines. When I was thirteen or fourteen, they had been sitting in his basement for years and years.

In 7 Mile, the claw machines were along a wall that was boarded up, along with a jukebox. The claw machine was filled with colored gravel—blue green, white red—and lying on the gravel

(Left) Metal animals from actual claw machines, circa 1930. To beat players at the claw machine game, Lenny used to weigh down the pot metal animals with molten lead, anchor them to the bottom of the glass cage, or file the claws so the animals would slip out of grasp.

were these animals made of metal—elephants, giraffes, lions, tigers. Each one of these animals had a value. So if you picked up a hippopotamus which is really hard because it was big and round, and drop it down the shoot, that'd be worth twenty-five bucks. You'd take the animal up to the bartender, and he'd give you twenty-five bucks.

My uncle had very nice machines. Some were really easy, like the giraffe; you could get ahold of its neck, and that might get you five bucks.

There were probably fifteen animals in each one of these claw machines. You'd have, like, two minutes, and if you didn't get an animal in two minutes, you'd have to drop another quarter in.

Now here's the sneaky part. To help keep the payouts low, these things would be done: These animals were made out of cast metal, pot metal. They were kinda heavy, probably weighed a pound, with a hole in the bottom. What they would do is they would pour lead in one side of the hole, and that

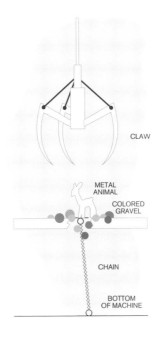

CLAW

METAL
ANIMAL

COLORED
GRAVEL

CHAIN

BOTTOM
OF MACHINE

THE CLAW MACHINES WERE ALONG A WALL THAT WAS BOARDED UP, ALONG WITH A JUKEBOX. THEY WERE FILLED UP WITH COLORED GRAVEL— AND LYING ON THE GRAVEL WERE THESE ANIMALS MADE OF METAL. ELEPHANTS, GIRAFFES, LIONS, TIGERS.

would off-balance the animal, so if you went to pick it up with the claw, it would slip out of the claw.

The other thing they did was that they would file the fingers of the claw till they were smooth so it couldn't grab really well.

And the worse part of the whole thing was, they would bury the animal about halfway in the gravel, and they would put a little chain on the foot, and anchor it on the bottom, so that if you started to pull it up, it would pull right out of the claw.

Now the glass on the machine was made out of safety glass—the kind of glass that, if you broke it, would break into a million pieces. Some of these guys would get so mad they couldn't win—and some were pretty big guys, truck drivers—they would just take their fists and smash the glass and try to break it. So my uncle started putting in material called herculite in there. It was the early forerunner of bulletproof glass, so when the guys would hit it, they'd break their wrists, not the glass.

After they were outlawed, my uncle made the decision that these claw machines were nothing

COUNTY OF SAN MATEO
COURTHOUSE • REDWOOD CITY • CALIFORNIA   № • 1219
OFFICE OF LICENSE COLLECTOR
EMERSON 9-1441
NEW ☐   RENEWAL ☐

NAME   Camille M. Stuehler   DATE   Jan. 9, 1961

ADDRESS   7 Mile House, Bayshore Blvd. at Geneva Ave.

Bayshore City, Calif.

Mechanical Play License

Pursuant to the provisions of ORDINANCE 752 of San Mateo County and upon payment of

$ __120.00__ (license fee), license is hereby granted the above person or persons to keep, carry on, conduct, transact or maintain in said County the business, occupation or calling of Mechanical Play

device or automatic Amusement device as the same is described in said Ordinance for __12__ months,

from the __1st__ day of __Jan. 1961__ to __Dec. 31, 1961__

Number of machines __Two__

License Collector of the County of San Mateo.

Customers at the 7 Mile House have played machines since the 1940s, starting with bandit-type slot machines. In the 1950s, they played Lenny's claw machines. I found an old mechanical play license that Camille obtained in 1961, meaning they had machines then even when she ran the bar. When I took over, there was a small TV-like game machine at the bar; the bartender would give payouts to winners. The old regulars asked if I would keep it; I didn't.

but junk, that there would never be a use for them again. One summer, I went in his basement and tore each one of those machines apart for scrap metal. We put all the brass aside in one pile, aluminum, copper…there was a lot of expensive metal in those machines.

One more nefarious thing my uncle was involved in was that he used to have a couple of bottles of each house liquor under the bar. One of them was straight, one was cut. If they had a guy sitting there at the bar getting toasted, getting drunk, they'd start serving him drinks out of the mix. I remember asking my uncle about that. "It doesn't make sense to me that there are two bottles, and both of them are being used." And he was pretty straightforward with me. He said, "You know when they have too much to drink, you don't want them to get so bad that they can't walk out of the place, so we start serving him out of this bottle."

But the thing was, they were still paying the same amount, whether or not it was cut. They were too far gone to notice.

Another interesting story was when my uncle took me to the Cow Palace. Every two months they'd have a big wrestling match there. So we saw these guys—and what I know is they all hate

ONE MORE **NEFARIOUS THING MY UNCLE WAS INVOLVED IN** WAS THAT HE USED TO HAVE A COUPLE OF BOTTLES OF EACH HOUSE LIQUOR UNDER THE BAR. **ONE WAS STRAIGHT, ONE WAS CUT.**

each other, and they're gonna break their necks. After the wrestling match was over, we stopped by 7 Mile House on our way home. And there they were—there must've been ten of the wrestlers who were at that match that evening. And they're sitting around at the bar buying each other drinks! My mouth dropped. I knew this guy hated that guy, and here they are slapping each other on the back! It was like discovering there was no Santa Claus. I was really hurt. That's one experience I'll never forget. For guys who looked like they wanted to kill people, they were really friendly.

My uncle went in the hospital for liver problems early '64. I remember when he started going downhill. I think he took me home and my mom said, "You know Len, you look terrible." His eyes were all yellow and he looked like he had a basketball in his belly. He had lost a lot of weight, he was tall, six-foot-two, six-three, but he was skin and bones. When he got out of the hospital, he would drink orange juice. Then he'd started mixing it with vodka, then he was back to where he was before. My dad said, "You know Len, if you don't stop this you're going to die. There's nothing else we can do for you. You're captain of your own ship."

My aunt wasn't a drinker. I think that was one of the reasons she filed for divorce. He would not stop his drinking. My aunt was very nice to us, and I think she just got fed up with Lenny's

WRESTLING
Cow Palace
SAT., MAR. 16
8:30 P.M.

Triple Main Event

For U.S. Title
STEVENS
vs.
CARPENTIER

For World's Tag Team
Championship
BOCKWINKLE
& SNYDER
vs.
NEILSON
BROS.
GOMEZ
vs.
THE SPOILER

Special Attraction
ELLIS
vs.
WRIGHT
3 Other Bouts

CRANE BOX OFFICE
STEINBERG SHOE STORE
COW PALACE

BIG TIME WRESTLING
COW PALACE—Sat., June 2nd 8:30 p.m.
DOUBLE MAIN EVENTS
WORLD TAG TEAM CHAMPIONSHIP
ARAKAWA   STEVENS
and   VS.   and
SHIBUYA   MANOUKIAN
champions   challengers
2 out of three falls—1 hour time limit
GOMEZ   NIELSON
and   VS.
MARTINEZ   BROS.
SPECIAL ATTRACTION
BEARCAT WRIGHT
VS.
KARL VAN SCHOBERG
1 fall—30 minute time limits
4 Other Bouts
CRANE BOX OFFICE * STEINBERG SHOE STORE
COW PALACE * SHERMAN CLAY BOX OFFICE, OAKLAND

Lenny was a doting uncle to his nephew, bringing him to wrestling matches at the Cow Palace.

shenanigans. I think they must've sold the house in Millbrae as part of the divorce settlement, and I'm not sure of the circumstances how Camille ended up with the bar.

My uncle passed away in 1965.

We were the closest that he had for family. I liked my uncle. He was a great guy. He was always good to me.

LENNY'S PASTA CON PESTO

ncle Lenny and I would go to the grocery store, and we would go in and buy a chicken from the rotisserie. He raised fresh basil—he loved to raise herbs—and we would make green spaghetti, *pasta con pesto*. I did not like it at first, but I worked hard over at his house—moving around stuff, mowing the lawn, and I was so hungry, that it was like if I didn't eat this green spaghetti, all I'm going to eat is chicken. Now, all of us in the family, we all love green spaghetti. My wife and I raise fresh basil, and we process it and save it for the winter months. That's because of my uncle. - *Rick Stuehler*

WHAT YOU NEED:
2-3 heaping tablespoonfuls of fresh basil leaves—use big leaves!
2-3 cloves garlic
stir in the blender with olive oil to a thin paste
throw in 3-5 tablespoons parmesan
stir again

Serve with rotisserie chicken.

Lenny's green spaghetti, recreated and photographed by Toni Zernik.

When we

DANCED

As told by

OLGA CALARZA *and* **DOLORES RODRIGUEZ**

Olga and her niece Dolores must have been absolutely alluring in their youth—Dolores, a statuesque fifteen, in her perfectly coiffed hair; Olga, eighteen, with her skirts swinging as she danced the night away. They started coming to the restaurant in the late Fifties, and speak of it as it was just yesterday. Their reminiscing easily transports you to their heyday, a time when innocence and propriety was a curious counterpoint to the carefree exuberance of the age.

OLGA: I used to come here from 1957 to 1960. I stopped after I had met my husband George. Every Friday and Saturday night, we used to go to a Mexican dances, and then after that, we'd come up this way. We didn't know whose car we were getting into, but in those days, it wasn't dangerous. I don't know how 7 Mile did it—it was a shack but it was always packed. There was always something good going on here. The dancing, the drinks, the jukebox...sometimes they'd have a little band. It was lively, but it wasn't rowdy. I was still available then. Then I saw my husband here. I said, "I'm going to make him mine, I'm going to make him mine." Later, I met him at the Copacabana on Broadway.

DOLORES: The Copacabana—everybody hung out there. There were three places with live music: 7 Mile, Babes Tower, and Log Cabin.

OLGA: The Civic Center used to have Mexican dances for us. The Ballroom Star. Then they started on Mission Street. I would save money for the weekend. Those dances were a dollar, or a dollar-fifty. No higher than three dollars, and they'd hire big orchestras. Hole-in-the-wall rinky bars—that was where everyone was going. Sometimes, you'd have American music like R&B. In 7 Mile it was mostly R&B. You'd find some Latin but not a lot. We dressed up—skirt, heels, pedal pushers, sweater, or a jacket. The men, too—jackets, slacks, not sloppy like today. We never got over drunk, we never got obnoxious, we didn't get loud. Even the "bad" girls then weren't bad. George thought I was a hoochie girl, because I chased after him, but when we got married, he found out. I just liked flirting around, but I wasn't bad." We went to all the bars, isn't that terrible? Half the people who came out here with us are probably gone already.

DOLORES: The women started getting married at fifteen, sixteen years old. The youngest who got married was thirteen. I married when I was fifteen. Boy, what a good provider my husband was. And also very handsome! I was married fifty years. Our group right now, the one that used to come here, are all going one by one. But we had good experiences here in 7 Mile; it wasn't like somewhere and you have people pulling out guns and everything.

OLGA: There was a lot of work here, factories. The men would stick around late and sometimes forget to go home. Truck drivers, locals who wanted to be with other guys. The number one organization then was the Teamsters. They'd have lunch, cross the street here to cash their checks, have a drink. I drank scotch and soda. It was fifty cents, and that was a lot of money. The owner was a woman, but she'd stand in the back. She'd be friendly, but she only talked to the guys whom she already knew. Kidding around, talking to them.

DOLORES: And the nationalities! They were all here. Olga's husband is Irish and Puerto Rican. My father's family was from Malacca, Spain. But in Texas, where we had come from, it was worse. They didn't like us because of the Alamo. But people who came here to 7 Mile had a different mental outlook on things. I don't think those issues were bothersome to them; they had a different outlook towards people and themselves. They were hardworking people.

OLGA: They all came here to have fun. To relax. Drink, dance, talk. It was very different from where we came.

DOLORES: My grandfather—Olga's father—brought us all out here from Texas. He worked at Southern Pacific.

OLGA: He brought eighteen of us here in 1947. He wasn't going to leave anyone behind. We lived in the ghetto in Texas, shacks and all that. It was called Barrio San Antonio; it's a freeway now. It was

AND WHEN WE GOT ON THE **TRAIN IN TEXAS**, HE TOLD US, **"TAKE A LAST LOOK AT THIS**...BECAUSE **YOU'LL NEVER SEE THIS UGLY RACIST TOWN AGAIN!"**

Dolores and Pete Rodriguez (left) and Olga and George Calarza (right). Niece and aunt, close in age, came to California from Texas, where Mexicans were still reviled due to the Alamo.

by the river, a poor area near the Alamo. My father did it because my brother-in-law liked to smoke marijuana and do drugs; my father thought that by bringing him here, maybe we can make a new life. Oh, we were ghetto. Everyone took drugs in that alley. Even today I ask my sister, "how can people have gotten drugs when they were all so poor?" She said, "They find ways."

My aunt asked my father to go to Ohio or Michigan; he said no. Then she said, "Come to California, see if you like it. I'll lend you the money, and you know, Southern Pacific is hiring." He came, and he brought three sisters—I have nine sisters and two brothers. He brought the three oldest ones. Dolores' mother was already married. He told her mother, "I'm taking all of them, even your husband, so if you wanna come...I'm not leaving one behind." And when we got on the train in Texas, he told us, "Take a last look at this...because you'll never see this ugly racist town again!"

DOLORES: I remember sitting in the train for three days. My grandfather brought my mother, my father, and my sister over and we took that train. We had to get the cheapest ticket and we had to sit for three days. I was in my mother's arms, and I remember, I was so tired. I wanted to lie down, and my mother would say, "We're almost there, Lolly, we're almost there."

OLGA: There were twenty-four people in our house in San Bruno. My father built three rooms. He was a jack of all trades. There were two bedrooms downstairs, and then the kitchen, and the porch, but we never felt that we were overcrowded. He bought it for three or four thousand dollars. He took what he got. My father said, "This is your house now, this is your home." No matter where we were, we all lived near each other.

DOLORES: When we got here, we lived downstairs. We had a room—my mother, my father, my sister and I, we had a crib that we shared. And then the other room had five boys, and in another room was another aunt with her children. Our male cousins would watch over us like little daddies. It was so tiny. But I never heard my grandmother say, "Oh you left dishes in the sink," or "You left your shoes outside." My grandfather would sleep downstairs, he would guard everyone so everything would be okay. We had a potbellied stove that he would turn on every night; he'd go down early and warm it up. We were so happy there.

OLGA: He had a flashlight to make sure everyone was safe. He was a wonderful father. My mother didn't want to leave Texas, she thought that was her home. My father said, "then you don't go, but I'm taking all my kids with me." So she had to go. We came in on the train and my brother went, "We're almost there! We're almost there" "Where? Where?" We couldn't wait to see where we were gonna go. And then it was the end of the line. At that time that was the biggest thing, the Southern Pacific Railroad. My father got a job right away; he was a porter and janitor. The stop was right in front of 7 Mile, and the train ran all the way up to Embarcadero. We were excited, but we didn't

George and Olga, and her sister Esther and husband Hank Leon. Esther and Hank started coming over in 2004, when I took over.

explore until later on. He kept us close. He loved us so much that he kept us close. It was a beautiful time.

DOLORES: But in that new neighborhood...I remember this woman had a daughter, and her daughter played with me. I could never go into her house because she was prejudiced. Her daughter never understood why I was never let into their house.

OLGA: One neighbor came over, not to be neighborly because she had her husband build her a beautiful big house, and ours was a shack. We invited her to come in, and she looked in, and she said, "Oh, you have a very clean house and your kids are very well dressed!" She would check us out. Maybe she thought that because we had so many people in our house, we lived in squalor.

DOLORES: Sometimes it wasn't about race. I was in junior high school, and I had a German and Mexican friend. The German asked my Mexican friend to come out and play, but not me. "No, not you." "Why?" "Because you're dark." So I went home and said, "I hate being dark! Give me some bleach!" Olga said, "Lolly, what's wrong with you?" I said, "I hate this color!"

OLGA: I told her, "You see this color? One day it's going to be in." I was about fifteen, and Dolores was thirteen.

DOLORES: But Texas was worse. Whites and blacks and Mexicans couldn't drink from the same drinking fountain. And when I was about three years old, I was about to sit in the front of the bus, and my mom said, "no you can't sit there." And I remember a tiny white woman gave me the dirtiest look like "how dare you sit there." I never could understand that. But our grandmother did not let us speak English in the house. I'm so happy she did that.

OLGA: At that time, I hated it. She used to say, "Outside. You leave it at the door. You don't bring it in here. No matter what, you're Mexican, and all you speak is Spanish."

DOLORES: But we were happy. We went to the Academy of Science, the Zoo, Playland. Everything was free. The museums, concerts in the park. My mom would pack a little picnic and bring us on a bus and that was our little weekend thing.

OLGA: There was a lot of racism growing up. But after 1958, it just started to change, it wasn't that bad anymore. I noticed it. They didn't say anything to me after that. I started working when I was seventeen; four hours of school, four hours of work. That's how we made our money because we wanted to have pretty clothes. I worked at Crest's on Mission St. where you could get hamburgers for thirty-three cents. That's when I started going to different areas. I was the type who would always investigate—"What's going on?" "What nationality are you?" We started exploring, going to the Cow Palace, seeing different people, getting together. There was no racism here in 7 Mile.

DOLORES: She was a lot of fun, she taught me how to drink beer.

OLGA: I taught her how to drink it with Coke. "Put a tall glass in the freezer, put the beer in, and wait. Watch, Lolly."

DOLORES: After I got married, I would come here to look for my husband or father-in-law. Olga always wanted to bring me along, but they drank so much, and I was worried about the kids. I had my first one at sixteen, second at seventeen. But I did come with my husband a couple of times here, because he wanted me to; I'd do the lunchtime thing but never the nighttime. He was a gentleman, so proper.

My father-in-law used to leave my son in the car when he'd go to 7 Mile. When he'd come out, his grandson would go "I've been here for a long time!" And my father-in-law would go, "Don't worry, I'll take care of you," and he always did. He gave him whatever he wanted. And my husband, he was the same—he took the mud, the blood, and the beer. Live fast, die young, and have a good-looking corpse. He was wild, oh boy. But he took very good care of us. He loved me so, in his own crazy way.

Esther (leftmost) brought in her sister, Olga and niece Dolores, after several decades of them not visiting 7 Mile. I'll forever regard that day as one of my luckiest; I never get tired of listening to their stories.

OLGA: It's nice to be here again. I'm sitting here and I look and remember. It's good to remember, to see and think and feel these things. When I come up this way, I point to 7 Mile and I tell my daughter, "those were the good times." And she'd say, "there you go again, Ma."

Yeah, those were my good times. I really enjoyed my life. I tell my kids, I have no regrets. I lived my life. Dolores married so young, she didn't get to do things. My kids tell me, "I wish I was born in your era. You had dancing, and everyone you were with was always dancing."

Love and equality at 7 Mile

We're all

FAMILY

here

As told by

PAUL PETE

Portrait by TONI ZERNIK, 2017

"The atmosphere makes us want to come back," Thelma Pete says of the warm service, good food, and music at 7 Mile House, where her husband Paul used to hang out as a young man. He stopped coming around fifteen to twenty years ago, and these days, it's their children—and children's friends—who like to come to enjoy what 7 Mile has to offer. But when they can, the Petes drop in for dinner or special occasions. When they're with family, their affection is so palpable. It's what drew me to approach them one day. I'm happy I did, and had the privilege to hear Paul Pete's story firsthand. Here it is.

My name is Paul Pete. I'm seventy-eight years old. I started coming here when I was seventeen. I was working two jobs—here in the union, and I was also working for Bimbo's nightclub. When I first started working for Bimbo's, I was parking cars, and then I became a doorman. I'm retired now but I used to work in this area for different companies for a long time. I worked in Consolidated Chemicals across the street—all the way to the hill over here. Its nickname was The Barnyard. I also worked for S&W Foods; they made See's Candies. And across right down from there on Bayshore was C&H Foods. All this was industrial and ILWU being a warehouse and longshore union, we had this all, this whole portion. I was in ILWU (International Longshore and Warehouse Union). Teamsters and ILWU were the two biggest unions. We ran the city, let's put it that way. We ran the *state*.

We were all together: You bothered one, you bothered all. We had strikes, we'd shut down the whole city. We was one big family. We were together raising all our kids, sending them to school, teaching them to stick to each other and respect each other, not like now that you got gangs and stuff.

We were young. We used to get our beer and alcohol here. Me, I'd bring my lunch if I was on the day shift. And we would cash our checks here. When we worked graveyard, some got off at six-thirty and some at seven in the morning, so banks weren't open yet, and if you were graveyard shift, your last day would be Friday morning. That's when our weekend started. So before going home and getting into bed, we just stopped here and cash our checks and go about our business. A lot of guys, they had accounts, the whole bit, so this was a very popular place for us. There was very nice times. Very popular place. Legal age for drinking? Twenty-one.

I was drinking beer, and also a little Jack Daniels. It was twenty-five cents for a beer. Some alcohol was about fifty cents, depends. I used to get two to three bags of groceries for two dollars. Food was cheap, gas was cheap, cars were cheap, everything was cheap then. The jukebox, it played R&B, rock and roll, blues and Western. A lot of country and Western music. I'd play BB King, Jackie Wilson, Johnny Cash. We loved music. We loved to dance and we'd sit around and talk and do steps and carry on. Live music came later in the '60s. There was a lot of women working with us, sure! We partied, all mingled. Girlfriend-boyfriend, everybody comin' here. We'd be laughing and talking and makin' friends.

For a while we was at the Silver Terrace in San Francisco. Our favorite club was Sam Jordan's, the one on Third Street, they're still there now, but we don't hang there anymore. That was in the Fifties. That was our place. Al Flynn? Yeah I remember Al Flynn, but there was a guy who did bookie too—Jessie Pratt. That was common back then. Gambling all kinds of ways.

It was mostly the bartenders running this place at that time. Once in a while we'd see Camille but basically we'd see the guys. On their breaks, they'd be coming in during the hours that it was open. You'd see all kinds of people. There was no fighting. We'd drink and stuff, arguin' about sports and different fights. We had some guys in the

The famous window, where Al Flynn or his trusted bartenders would slip vast amounts of cash to Teamsters or men from ILWU.

89

The historic Sam Jordan's still stands today. It was established in 1959.

union who were professional fighters. We'd talk but we'd never let that get to the point of getting physical. Everybody I know knows this is a place where they can come and relax. There weren't too many blacks visiting here then. But a lot of whites and a few Mexicans. They had another place up the street, where the Dollar Store at. We all mingled, we was all one big family.

I came to California when I was eleven or twelve. I was born in Louisiana, in my grandmother's house. Then we lived in Houston, Texas, and then I left Houston and came to California. I had developed asthma, and they said the climate here is better for my health. I stayed with my mother's sister and her husband. That's how I got started, with them. I've had a pretty colorful exciting life. Texas and Louisiana, it didn't make any difference. I have survived the Ku Klux Clan, all that stuff. The Ku Klux Clan, they hurt my grandfather. My grandfather, for a black man, done well for

I'VE HAD A PRETTY **COLORFUL EXCITING LIFE. TEXAS AND LOUISIANA,** IT DIDN'T MAKE ANY **DIFFERENCE.** I HAVE SURVIVED **THE KU KLUX CLAN.**

Thelma and Paul Pete. They drop in occasionally for dinner, or when their children or children's friends have something to celebrate.

himself. He came out of Canada and he had property back then, and they decided they wanted some of this property and he wouldn't sell it. They snatched him one night and tried to make him sell it. He wouldn't, so they cut his arms off. He never fully recovered from it. So that woke me up to understand what that was all about. From then on, I was a different person. I was a young boy, but it all hit because they were teaching us how to survive. And so, you know, from then, I had to grow up real fast and always remember how to take care of my family.

See, California has a sophisticated racism. And over the years, I see them exploit people of all colors. They pit them against each other, and it hasn't stopped. When I was young, they didn't have a lot of Asians, but we were all very close, we let each other in each other's house. You see everybody, even the kids—we took them places; we helped take care of the house; two or three of us, we'd take each other's kids to the beach or whatever so the women could have their time to relax. But as time went on — the Sixties, Seventies, Eighties — you saw them divide against each other. Gangs, killing. People started moving out of the area. On my block, I been there forty-six years. On one block, we were one family. Today, I know three families on that block. They don't even speak. You know, you gonna say "good morning, how you doing," and they ignore you. It makes you miss a lot of things. All we fought for just to get to this point…now, we the bad people.

I miss all the guys and all the places that was here. I wonder what happened to them. I've lost contact. I've always had a lot of good time fun here. I be workin' here, some workin' right over there, but we were all in the same union, demanding the same thing. We'd see each other two to three times a week and we'd be huggin' and carrying on and buying drinks. It was a family thing. It was *family* here.

Spilling a drink

and falling in

LOVE

As told by

LUCILLE STONE

Quite a number of people met their lifetime partners at 7 Mile. One of these lucky people is Lucille Stone, who was dating another man at the time her future husband literally bumped into her in 1965. Bob passed away in 2016, and Lucille visited 7 Mile House a year after to reminisce. She was ecstatic to find some things unchanged (like the bathroom doors), and some things improved (like the food). Her biggest thrill was seeing that we had preserved the railroad ties out front, where she and Bob sat and spent hours talking after he spilled his drink on her, and sealed their fate.

ob and I met fifty-one years ago at the 7 Mile. Those were the good ol' days. I had just turned nineteen, and used to work at the Cow Palace as a spare time job. Mainly I worked downtown in San Francisco. My girlfriend and I used to come in on a streetcar, and my boyfriend Harold would pick us up and we'd come here. It was a little neighborhood bar that you just went to to talk and do a little dancing, and everybody knew everybody. It was just a relaxing place, and we had a lot of fun. I used to tease him, "Really fancy place, Harold!"

I remember Harold's friend, the bartender, dancing with me, and he asked, "how old are you?" I said, "Well, how old do you think I am?" "Feels twenty-three," he said. "Well that's a good age!" I said. I left it at that, so he thought I was twenty-three. I *did* have a phony I.D.

There was a jukebox—we were playing rock and roll, mostly. I only got into country and Western when I met my husband. I was either drinking Screwdrivers or vodka and grapefruit juice. Then I danced and it made me lose weight. I used to love to dance. I don't remember any food being served.

I knew Harold was married. As I was growing up, I was a good girl. I said I would not purposely go with a married man. I always told myself, "Why am I hanging with a married person? I wasn't going to take him from his wife; I don't have the time for that!" But it wasn't a love affair or anything, we were just having drinks.

So one day, me and Harold and my girlfriend Donna went to 7 Mile, and we sat at this U-shaped booth right by the restroom. I had just come from work downtown and had my nylons on

Bob and Lu Stone in October of 1966 (far left), and in November 2015 (above). The photo on the opening page was taken on their wedding day, January 27, 1966.

and everything, all the good stuff. This guy spilled a drink on me! And I just kinda laughed and I said, this is where I go to the bathroom. I went to wipe myself up a little bit. His name was Bob and he was so embarrassed. He thought I was going to yell at him, but I didn't yell and the next thing I know, we were outside sitting on the little curb, talking for hours and hours and hours. I was never a talker, especially with strangers. But we were sitting right there at the end of the building. I don't even know what we were talking about.

And that was my husband. I met him there at 7 Mile.

Harold didn't mind when I started dating Bob. My girlfriend started hanging out with him, she ended up marrying him, and he got a divorce. And I married Bob and we're all still friends today. But my husband passed away on May 23, 2016. We were married for fifty years, and he made it to his seventy-fifth birthday and our fiftieth wedding anniversary in January. We have three beautiful children, twelve grandchildren, and two great grandchildren.

Visiting 7 Mile—it just made my day. My daughter said to me when I came home, "Aww, you really had a good time huh?" "Yeah," I told her. "It was nice."

NO HOME
BUT BRISBANE

Mile House has the peculiar distinction of being at the cusp of three cities: San Francisco, Daly City, and Brisbane. Coming up on Bayshore Boulevard, Daly City limits end just at the corner of the mechanic/auto repair shop, which shares the same lot on which 7 Mile House stands. I had trouble with our address up until the early 2000s. Its location brought about contention regarding our official address: 2800 Bayshore Boulevard, Brisbane CA 94005 was our *business* address, while 2800 Bayshore Boulevard, Daly City, CA 94014 was our *mailing* address. Why? Because the Brisbane Post Office said it was too far for them to deliver to us. It was cumbersome, to say the least, having to explain to each and every one of my contacts why I had two addresses. Thankfully, I managed to convince the Brisbane Postmaster to include us in their route.

Up until the Sixties, many considered 7 Mile House part of San Francisco, as the boundaries of that city and the yet-to-be incorporated Brisbane still had to be clarified. In 1963, when Brisbane was already a city, some citizens of the Bayshore neighborhood proposed that the residential area of Bayshore and the Cow Palace be annexed to Daly City. This just added more confusion.

The possibility of incorporating Brisbane as a city was first brought up in the 1950s, but rejected. In the meantime, factories, livestock yards, and stockyards around the area continued to operate. Rick Stuehler describes a rather macabre occurrence that arose from the dystopian night scene from the era: "That was a scary area at night. You'd see the bums, homeless guys roaming around, so it was not a place at night to go except for the railroad guys. Nobody bothered them. It was the edge of the civilization. There used to be a dairy up the street past the Southern Pacific railyards. They brought those great big containers there, and they put milk in those containers, four feet tall stainless steel, to pasteurize. There was a gas station too across 7 Mile up towards north, and the winos used to hang out there at night. If these guys didn't have money to buy cheap wine, they used to go to the gas station and pour what was left in the hose, and they would mix it with milk from the dairy. I remember my dad and my uncle talking about this one guy that came into the bar

Brisbane in the 1950s.

and collapsed on the floor, and he was bleeding from his eyes and ears. He had been drinking this combination of milk and gasoline."

7 Mile House still stands on the edges, across a landfilled area that used to be a bay where pirates stashed their loot and bootleggers silently coasted along, transporting their liquor. But nights on Bayshore Boulevard are no longer as frightening, and Brisbane—now called "The City of Stars," erstwhile called the "The City That Grew Out of the Depression" and "The City With a Heart"—was incorporated in 1961. We at 7 Mile House—residents since 1858—like to call it "home."

4

....

HALF A CENTURY
OF THOSE
HALCYON DAYS

THE SOFTER SIDE OF A 'TOUGH PIECE OF MEAT'; BOOKIES, BARTENDERS, AND WAR VETERANS; LOST RECIPES AND UNFORGETTABLE BURGERS (1966 – 2003)

What do we know of Camille Marie Mueda, née Stuehler, née Flynn, née Faccini, outside of facts published in public records? Not very much.

She was born on November 2, 1916 (some records say 1918) to Jessie Kelly and Vincent Henry Faccini, a homemaker and a chauffeur, in San Francisco. The two met in North Beach—an Italian enclave—before the great earthquake of San Francisco. Italian-Irish co-marriages were common then, due to both being predominantly Catholic.

Camille had an older sister, Irene, and brother, John Henry, born in 1907 and 1911, respectively. Irene married and became Irene Delucca, and died in 1977. John Henry served in the war as a private in the medical department, and died in 1964, around the time Camille was getting a divorce from Lenny Stuehler. Camille's father died in 1954; her mother, in 1967.

She married young—either at sixteen or eighteen, depending what birth year you believed—in 1934, and had her firstborn, Leslie Albert Flynn, Jr., in the very same year. Seven years later, she

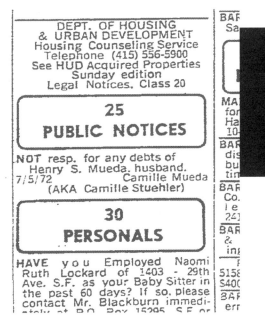

Camille in her signature hairdo in the 1960s; a public notice in the San Francisco Chronicle *on July 7, 1972 included a posting from Camille not being responsible for any of her husband's debts. (Previous page) A Polaroid of 7 Mile House's old facade.*

had another son, whom she named Dennis Gerald. It's not clear when she divorced Leslie Albert, Sr., but when she did, her son Albert dropped the "Leslie" from his name. A good estimate is the mid-Forties, as she is listed as Camille Stuehler, spouse of Leonard Stuehler, by 1948 in California directories.

As we mentioned in the prior chapter, she divorced Lenny in 1964. He passed away in 1965, making her sole proprietor of 7 Mile House. Camille remarried in 1969, this time to a Massachusetts

Building Up In Brisbane

New building in Brisbane last month totaled $80,512, city secretary Paulette Torvik reported today.

Permits issued were to William Montgomery, $1,690, addition to residence at 205 Kings Road; Paul Schmidt, $19,790, dwelling at 131 Alvarado Street; Michael Castiglia, demolition at 2852 Bayshore Boulevard.

Roger Repp, $829, addition at 121 Kings Road; R. Cedsky, $2,000, alteration at 100 Trinity Road; Alice Wimmer, $3,750, addition at 261 Mendocino Street; H. H. Brady and W. Wollentson, $4,500 new building at 701, 713 and 733 San Bruno Avenue.

Roger Merritt, $200, alteration at 113 San Benito Road; Lawrence Frugoli, $900, alteration at 2800 Bayshore Boulevard; Brisbane School District, $2,700, alteration on Solano Street, and $6,631, alteration on San Bruno Avenue.

In 1967, Lawrence Frugoli made alterations to the 7 Mile House, as announced in the San Mateo *Times* on August 29 of the same year.

native named Henry "Hank" Santos Mueda. They were wed in a civil ceremony in Reno, Nevada. Old 7 Mile House regulars and employees from the Eighties and Nineties say they did not separate, despite Hank's obvious abuse.

"He'd come down here, set up the bar, get ice, put money in his pocket…you know," one old bartender says with a shrug. "Camille ended up with no money. He took it all. But they never separated. He died first."

Hank passed away in 1994 in Daly City. By that time, Albert "Al" Flynn had stepped in and was overseeing much of the bar's operations for his mother, who was well into her seventies. By then, she was also well into her cups—a stark difference from her sober days in the 1950s and 1960s, since, as Rick Stuehler describes, "my aunt wasn't a drinker." (However, Mercedes Virzi, who was married to Al in the Fifties, says that Camille was already fond of her libations even then.)

Either way, Camille was a tough old bird; "a tough piece of meat," the same old bartender calls her. She had survived the war, one abusive marriage, and two severe beatings during robberies in the Seventies and Eighties. The first was when she was just opening shop. It was 6 a.m., and thieves had crawled in through the bathroom window. Bars in the window were installed shortly after that, and opening time was moved to a more manageable 8 a.m. The second time, she was with her husband. "They took a shot at him as

Camille was a tough old bird, but could be quite maternal, especially towards her female employees and young customers. Here she is preparing a buffet for customers in the 1990s.

he ran out the door, but they had her," the bartender narrates.

Sometimes, I think of what Camille endured — by choice or by chance — when I'm faced with difficult times, business-related and otherwise. Sure, she grew up in a different time, was presented with wholly different life options — but is there any difference in the confusion, sadness, or rage that a woman feels when her heart gets broken, or when a loved one passes away? Are there shades to the pain of betrayal? How deep are the nuances when one feels utter loneliness or vulnerability?

My ex-husband, Roel Villacarlos, and I separated in 2011, thereabouts. We had put up the restaurant together seven years before that, but he always had his day job to fall back on. All I had was 7 Mile House. Though my family at 7 Mile at that time was already as amazing and supportive as they are now, I could not help but feel an almost physical sort of fear — what if I failed, what if people stopped coming? What if the choice I had made — to bank everything on this endeavor — was a mistake? We had a long way to go before being voted Best Hinterlands Bar of 2017. San Franciscans still had to consider us a "must-visit." I was in between homes, couldn't yet decide if my kids were going to go to the same school that year, and my credit record was abysmal.

But surely, I was — *am* — made of sterner stuff. I thought of all the years Camille put into this place–alongside Lenny, she had given it half a century! — and the ignominies she must've faced just to make sure 7 Mile House survived. If she could get through all that nonsense and chaos, and still keep the business intact, then certainly I could, too. We *de facto* single moms have great reserves of strength and perseverance.

I wish I had met her. Some people say she was nice; some say she was a force to contend with. Everyone, however, agrees that she was a character. She was a lady born and bred in a more gentle and proper time—always nicely dressed, made sure she always had earrings on (who was it that said a woman is never fully dressed without earrings?), hair done, makeup in place, and nails done—but her demeanor was that of one who'd been to hell and back. It was a combination you couldn't forget.

John Walsh, an ex-S.E. Rykoff driver who hung out in 7 Mile from 1974 to 1999, still remembers how she would size up people at the bar, and make the humorous but unreasonable request of having them thrown out. "I'd buy her a drink and sometimes, she'd get so stoned and say, 'John, who's that sitting at the end of the bar?' 'I don't know, Camille,' I'd answer. 'Get him the hell out,' she'd say, 'I don't like him. Get him out!'" John laughs at the memory. "I'd say, 'I can't do that, Camille!' Then she'd say, 'okay, I'll get Al to get his ass out. I don't like the guy.' And her profanity! Ooof." Now eighty-two, John talks with the careful, shaky inflection of an old man. To hear him giggle at the memory is pure delight. "If she liked you, you were in. But if she didn't like you, you weren't stayin' in there. It was the way she looked at a person I guess. She could tell if they were a good person or a bad person. Camille was very old fashioned."

"She was a tough woman, boy," Joni Walker, whose mother Anna married Al Flynn in the Sixties, and who tended bar at 7

More treasures from yesteryear: a booklet of check vouchers, most probably used for when unionists came and cashed their checks; a cash ledger in Camille's neat, flowy handwriting; one of Camille's old business cards; and the nameplate on her desk.

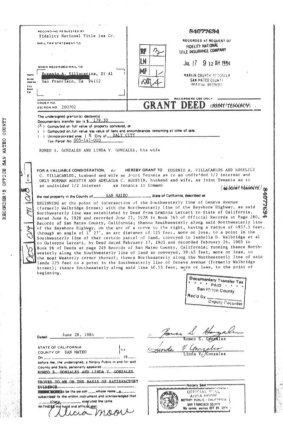

In 1984, Orly and Adelaida Agustin and Eugene and Roselily Villacarlos, as joint owners, bought the Bayshore corner Geneva lot from Romeo and Linda Gonzales.

IF SHE COULD GET THROUGH ALL THAT NONSENSE AND CHAOS, SURELY I COULD, TOO. WE DE FACTO SINGLE MOMS HAVE GREAT RESERVES OF STRENGTH AND PERSEVERANCE.

Mile in the Eighties, intones. "She was a touuuggghhh woman. I guess at that age and in those times, she never really thought about people's feelings when she said somethin'." Camille was a strict boss—even more so when the vodka over ice she was having would begin to take over. "Then she'd get loud. 'How come you haven't done your dishes?' 'You don't have glasses!' She'd get all nitpicky and it'd interrupt your system and how you worked," Joni remembers. "She'd be pleasant till about three in the afternoon. Then it was time for her to go."

For all her seeming meanness, however, Camille had a soft heart for her female employees. "She wouldn't allow women to work night shifts," Joni says. "You wouldn't have wanted a woman getting on a bus or train from that area. I think it was good-minded of her to do that."

She was also nice to kids. Ron Lee Moore, whose father Kenneth used to tend bar in the late

Sixties, remembers how Camille would watch over and ply him and his brother with sodas while they waited for their father to end his shift.

When Filipino couples Orly and Linda Agustin and Eugenio and Roselily Villacarlos took over as her landlords in 1984, Camille even helped them appeal to the Brisbane Planning Commission to get a fence erected around part of the property where the mechanic shop is located. "She was very nice. She appeared before the Commission for us," Orly says. "She told them she couldn't believe that they couldn't get the fence to us because of what happened to her before — she was mugged twice and the people who mugged her were hiding between the cars parked outside, in the open. We got our permit in the end."

Camille also never allowed 7 Mile to become a "biker bar," as has been alleged many times in newspaper articles. "It wasn't a Hell's Angels place. The Teamsters had bikes, but it was never a biker bar, no," Joni stresses. "Al and Camille would never have said yes to that."

Richard Huertas, who was a part-time bartender in the Eighties, describes Camille as "cool, a drinker." Echoing John Walsh, he says, "her spot was right there at the end of the bar," pointing a huge, tattooed arm towards where Camille sat. Her focus was on the cash register, and another bartender named Jebbie, on whom she kept a sharp eye. "But when she would drink too much," continued Richard, "her attitude would not be good."

Her tirades sometimes had the opposite effect. Instead of scurrying in fear, her crew would egg it on. Benny Hernandez, 7 Mile's most popular living bartender, says he and Poli Policarpio, a Filipino with a bad mullet who worked as a janitor, would water down Camille's drinks for fun — and laugh when she'd notice and scream at them for it.

Camille almost sold the liquor license (and therefore, ownership of the bar) to Richard's father Emilio for $125,000 in the Nineties, but the deal fell through. "She just wanted to get out," Richard recalls. She passed away in 2005, and her obituary reads, "owner of Seven Mile for over fifty years."

Her "way out" while she was still living was her son Al, who managed the bar and used it as an informal office for his illegal sports betting business. Al Flynn was Ronald "The Cigar" Sacco's main man on the West Coast.

While we could not find anyone who would go on the record about Ronnie Sacco and his associates at 7 Mile House, we did find an interview clip from CBS' *60 Minutes* on YouTube. In the episode, aired July 18, 1993, Steve Kroft sits down with Sacco and talks about his business. The

Camille and Benny—an iconic pair in their own right—at their designated places at the end of, and behind, the bar.

episode also includes interviews with government informants Fred Valis and Danno Hanks, who uploaded the clip himself on his YouTube channel.

Also in the interview is Jim Moody, head of the Organized Crime Section of the FBI at the time, who called Sacco "the top bookmaker in operation." Apparently, Sacco made around $100-million a month, or up to $50-billion a year. He was therefore the biggest and most successful bookie in history, with most of the money made from football and basketball games.

He was "king of the bookmakers," say Valis and Hanks. They had firsthand experience dealing with Sacco, as they posed as mechanics who knew how to install "untraceable" phone lines for the operation. They also acted as collectors and couriers, and, although accepted payment from the government as informants, also admit to having charged Sacco for imaginary expenses. For their duplicity, Sacco and his associates gave them the nicknames "Pestilence" and "Vermin"—names they find amusing. For all the animosity, though, Valis and Hanks acquiesced that Sacco ran a tight operation. Sacco, they said, set up a system that was "master charged." It was organized, and Sacco

Steve Kroft interviewed Ron "The Cigar" Sacco in a July 18, 1993 episode of *60 Minutes*.

was a "bookie with a vision."

Maybe this was because Sacco saw his business as that—a legitimate business, just like stockbrokering. You paid customers what they were due, with money made from commissions, or, in bookie parlance, "juice, vigorish, or vigor." Customers, in turn, paid their debts. Valis and Hanks said people who were involved in betting with bookies tended to be more upfront with paying their debts than paying their mortgage.

There was also talk of Sacco being involved with the Mafia, which he denied vehemently because the mob wouldn't get into anything "where they would lose money," and all they did was "take." Kroft brought up the fact that the Gambino family of New York had telephoned Sacco, asking him to be their bookie. The fearsome Gambino clan at that time was led by John Gotti, who was convicted of murder and racketeering a year before the *60 Minutes* episode came out. Sacco said he wasn't even sure if the call was indeed from the Gambinos, and that if ever the Mafia approached him, he would "run." FBI Agent Moody countered that it was unlikely Sacco *didn't* have any sort of protection from the mob, as the mob never allowed any national operation to run without their consent—or a cut.

How did Sacco's operation go? If you wanted to make a bet, it went like this: You had to know one of his agents. Like "a bartender, or a cashier in a café," explains Kroft in the episode. The agent would arrange a credit line for you, or how much you could bet. Then, he'd give you an account

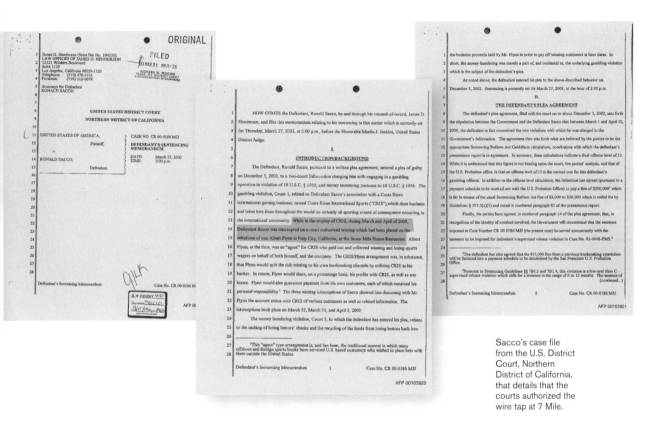

Sacco's case file from the U.S. District Court, Northern District of California, that details that the courts authorized the wire tap at 7 Mile.

number and a 1-800 number to call to place the bet.

For Sacco and his associates, deposits and withdrawals were not made at banks, but "dental labs, union halls, restaurants…" enumerates Valis in the interview. For the *60 Minutes* episode, Mission Jewelry & Loan Pawnbrokers in the Mission District was singled out. The proprietor, Daryl Kaplan, admits to having cashed checks for bookmakers, which he believes is not illegal. But the government alleged that he was also their banker, having made up to $80-million through the Sacco bookmaking operation. Consequently, Kaplan's pawnshop was raided. Kaplan said that the money

Al Flynn and his associates arranged bets from a phone booth in 7 Mile.
Here's an artist's rendition of where the phone booth was located.

FBI took was the pawnshop's money, and not what Sacco made from bookmaking.

To escape the heat, Sacco moved his operations offshore, to the Dominican Republic. He was arrested there in 1993, and while he was in jail, operations moved to Margarita Island, Venezuela, and then to Costa Rica. Upon his release, Sacco was hired as consultant to Costa Rica International Sports, or CRIS. From 1998 until 2002, he was head of CRIS, the most formidable online gambling brand in the world. In 2002, he was arrested for having two passports. An article in onlinebetting. com goes:

"On March 2, 2002 officials at the border post of Peñas Blancas Costa Rica discovered a man

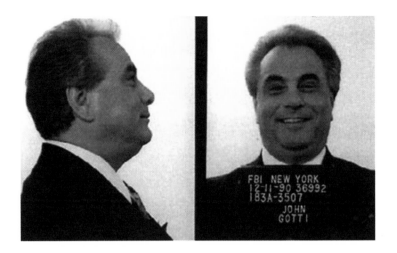

John Gotti's mugshot. Gotti was the head of the Gambino family of New York, who allegedly called Sacco to ask him to be their bookie. Sacco denied all ties with the mafia.

BUT THERE WAS SOMETHING ABOUT THEM— SACCO, AL, AND A SICILIAN NAMED LITTLE RONNIE, WHO SERVED AS THEIR RUNNER— THAT MADE PEOPLE AWARE THAT THEY WERE "A BIG DEAL."

entering Costa Rica carrying two passports with the same man photographed. One passport was issued in Los Angles to a U.S. citizen named Ronald Sacco, and the second issued in Belize to Ronald O'Malley who was listed as a naturalized citizen born in Ireland. After contacting the FBI it was discovered that Sacco was wanted in the United States for 2000 indictment in San Francisco on Bookmaking charges and was considered a fugitive. A short while later he was arrested with the crime being his use of two passports. In 2002, while others were celebrating freedom on the fourth of July, Ronald Sacco was deported to the United States."

Sacco pleaded guilty before a United States District Court in the district of Northern California on March 27, 2003.

Anna (in black) and her daughters, Toni (left) and Joni (right), with Al Flynn when he was hale and hearty in the early 1990s. (Below) A ticket to his Get Well fundraiser for Al, who contracted stomach cancer, later in the decade.

Richard Huertas says he actually met Sacco while the bookie king frequented the area, and was surprised when he saw him on TV one night. "I know that guy!," he remembers saying. Richard says Sacco visited 7 Mile House once a month before he returned to Costa Rica. He also went to the Pinch Hit Club, where Richard also tended bar. "He was a cool guy, he wasn't a big gangster type. He just wanted to do what he had to do. An average guy, wasn't dressed fancy. He had a brown leather jacket, a cigar. A '65 Mustang was what he had. That was it."

But there was something about them—Sacco, Al, and a Sicilian named Little Ronnie who served as their runner—that made people aware that they were "a big deal." Richard shrugs. "That's the way it is, you know when somebody stands out." Even the way Al took calls was distinct. "Al would give a little jerk," he describes, pulling back his shoulders and shimmying. "Like he liked what he was hearing. Then he'd go in the back, come out, and give someone their money."

Anna Southwick, Joni Walker's younger sister, describes the feeling she would get when people approached Al at the bar. He gave off a "Godfather" sort of aura, she says. "That's exactly it—when people walked in to talk to him, they waited their turn to talk to him. In his stern way, he told them what he wanted done. I never eavesdropped, but that's the way I saw it as well—he was like The Godfather. You never wanted to cross him, that's always the feeling I got."

Mother and son team. Camille and Al in the mid- to late 1970s. Al helped his mother,
and he helped the customers at 7 Mile when they were short on cash.

An interviewee for this book — let's call her Sheryl — says Al ran bets for Sacco that were made from a phone booth in 7 Mile House. The phone booth is long gone. No one we interviewed knows who took it. Sheryl was quick to add that while Al used the bar as his front, he kept his businesses separate. "He ran books, but what the Feds got from the bar wasn't the money he made (on the betting). That was 7 Mile's money," Sheryl says. "We only found out about his gambling activities when the FBI raided the bar," recalls Orly Agustin. "I was so surprised! There were so many cars, I couldn't even enter the property. They took the whole cash register but didn't find much cash."

Richard may have seen Al take out some cash from the back room, but most of it was for cashing checks. He charged a dollar for every hundred, says Joni. As was done in the 1950s, all the union men from the area "banked" at the 7 Mile. "The drivers went there, the warehousemen too," says John Walsh. "Al used to say, 'I hope I got enough money to cash all the checks.' Sometimes he wouldn't have enough. But he always cashed mine. He helped Camille, and he helped us. Al was good people."

Michael Tomola, another former S.E. Rykoff employee who became a regular in the late Seventies, likewise observed the tremendous amount of cash flowing from the back room. "We were paid once a week and were making too much money for young men, in my opinion. Fifteen-sixteen bucks an hour, back when minimum wage was probably three dollars an hour. We would go in Friday with our paychecks, fifty to sixty warehousemen, to cash our checks. Then the drivers, then other guys from another union would come in and cash their checks. All encashments. There had to be *a lot* of money in there."

Those were two things Al cherished as a person and as a businessman: Relationships and trust. Sheryl says that Al didn't like hearing anything that wasn't his business. "He didn't want to hear no gossip about anyone. That's what we did to earn trust. It's what you did to make people want to talk to you." And, suffice to say, as was mentioned in the *60 Minutes* interview, any bet made was a "gentleman's bet. You make a bet, you pay the bet," she explains. "If you don't know that, then don't get into the business. You're a welch."

But Al was a gangster—if you could call him that—with a heart. He treated Anna and Joni— and indeed, all their siblings—like his own, spending time with them and regaling them with his largesse. Anna saw him as a tender, if somewhat awkward and comical presence. He had a slight hunch to his shoulders, she remembers. He liked to rest one foot on the bar step as he spoke to her, and lean forward on his elbow, nodding "yeah, yeah."

"If you didn't know Al and sat with him at the bar, you'd think he was a hard-ass. But I remember sitting at the bar with him and we'd be sitting there watching football. He would tell me what was going to happen before the play would happen. I used to think he was psychic! Or he told them what to do, and they'd do it," Anna says, laughing at how gullible she was then. "The way he looked at you, the way he wobbled his head when he talked to you, it was funny."

Despite the wiseguy-speak and mien, "he probably lost more than he made," Sheryl remarks. "A lot of people owed him money. He would do anything for anybody." Al wore an ankle bracelet for a time, then fell ill and grew frailer and frailer by the day. According to Sheryl, by that time, Sacco had let him go. On October 29, 2009, he succumbed to stomach cancer at the age of seventy-five, shuttering the latest chapter in the colorful history of the Bay Area's last original mile house.

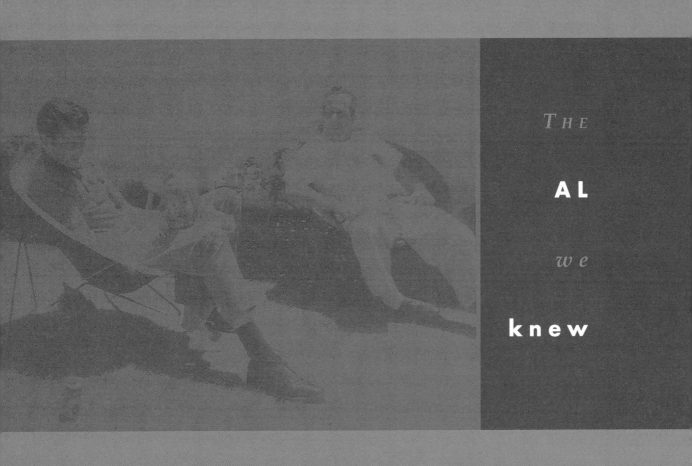

Mrs. Stuehler and her son, Al Flynn

THE

AL

we

knew

Mrs. Stuehler and her son, Al Flynn

He did it

HIS WAY

As told by

MERCEDES VIRZI

Portrait by TONI ZERNIK, 2017

117

What a head-turning pair Mercedes Virzi and Albert Flynn must've been! Two tall, dark haired good-looking kids—she, poised and reserved, he, powerful and charismatic. Today, Mercedes is just as arresting, with her shock of curly, black hair and quiet, gracious bearing that reminds you of old Hollywood stars. My first brush with her was when old business records of 7 Mile House were being passed on to me; I thought she was aloof and a tad intimidating. I was pleasantly surprised when I spoke to her for this book, and found her quite warm and willing to share her memories of Al. I was even more surprised when I learned she is part Filipino, which underscores how huge a role diversity and inclusivity plays in the story of 7 Mile House.

met Albert in high school. A lot of kids joined the service during the Korean war. The army hit up kids in high school here to join, and they all got swept up in it, and that's how Albert got in. He was only eighteen or nineteen when he was in the service.

I used to go to his grandmother's all the time. I really liked his grandma. She was crippled with arthritis. Her hands were so crooked. She didn't go out of the house, but she was very nice. He had a younger brother, Dennis, who had special needs. Camille had also left Dennis with Gram to take care of. Both were raised by Gram. Dennis went to live with Camille only when Gram died, and he was already grown by then.

I wasn't really raised with my family, as well. It was wartime and I went into the convent during the Forties—St. James on Guerrero Street. I married Albert when he came back in 1954 for his grandfather's funeral. Camille was in her thirties then. I was around eighteen when I got married. He was a good-looking kid, stood six-feet-two. Everybody liked Albert. We got married at Saint Michael's church up in Daly City. I was a nice-looking girl in my day, too, so...we just got married too young, and by the time we got married, we had nothing more to say to each other.

His life was: he was a Teamster, he worked at the 101 Truck Station, which was across the street from 7 Mile, but he'd be in the bar all the time, then he'd come home. Albert also went to another bar, a bar downtown for cops. That was his life. He left me two or three times; when he'd get angry, he'd just leave and go home to his mother. It was just hard to stay together, it really was.

Mercedes Virzi in 1952, and Al Flynn in 1960—a remarkably good-looking pair.
(Opening spread) Al with son Michael, around 1960, as Mercedes' uncle, Pete Virzi, looks on.

I realized I could raise two kids on my own, and he helped support them all their lives but we couldn't stay married (our daughter Lisa died early).

He never took the kids out once. His thing was to protect and provide. He always said that men were responsible for two things—support and taking out the garbage, and that's exactly what he did. He used to drink a lot and I didn't at all, I never liked the taste of it. We were quite the opposites. I was the girl who used to go to mass every day; he'd drop me off at church and would take me and leave me at the movies.

I didn't really go in the bar, and Albert didn't approve of women in bars anyway. What I know

BUT **HIS FAMILY** SAID **SOMETHING** TO HIM, SOMETHING LIKE THEY LIKED ME BUT THEY WOULD HAVE PREFERRED THAT HE MARRIED **"SOMEONE OF HIS OWN KIND."** WHEN THAT WAS SAID, HE WAS JUST AS STUBBORN. THAT'S WHAT **PUSHED HIM, AND ME TOO,** INTO **GETTING MARRIED.**

of it was that it was a truck stop, whatever women went in were women he didn't think very much of. It just wasn't a hangout for women, that's all I know. He was very old fashioned in that way.

Getting married to Albert had a lot to do with—aside from him being a cute looking kid—being pushed to do it. Albert and I, we loved each other, I would have to say that, but marriage was something *he* brought up, and something we could've been persuaded not to do. I wanted to go to city college at that time. But his family said something to him, something like they liked me but they would have preferred that he married "someone of his own kind." When that was said, he was just as stubborn. That's what pushed him, and me too, into getting married.

I'm Italian on my mother's side, and my father's Visayan (belonging to a group of islands

Magdaleno Refre, seated in the foreground, Mercedes' father, was a Filipino. He was a Visayan who was born in the Panay islands. Seated third from Magdaleno is Al. (Opposite page) Mercedes with daughter Lisa.

in the Philippines). He came here in 1932 maybe. His name was Magdaleno Refre, from the Panay Islands. My daughter and I took daddy back to the Philippines when he was in his eighties. We have terrific relatives there. My dad died when he was almost a hundred years old, and my mother died at ninety-three, ninety-four.

It wasn't wonderful growing up then. My mother always called me a half breed. She said that she and my father couldn't go out in the daytime and be seen together. In Chinatown, they were more accepted, and they did go out while they were there, but they stayed in Chinatown. I was born on North Point Street in an apartment in North Beach. Before the war, we lived on Green Street, but I don't recall my parents being together. My father liked to gamble and my momma said that he gambled away all her rent money. It was hard. They weren't married anyway, but she told me once, as she was walking up the street—it was normal practice then to sit out front on the stairs—these two women were talking and one of them spit at her. I asked her what she did, and she said, "I went into the house and I pulled the shades down."

My mannerisms are more Italian. I was born in North Beach, but I was raised with different families. During that period, you couldn't marry outside of your race. The Exclusion Act was still in effect. I was born in 1935 (the Act was repealed in 1943). My mom was once arrested on the street because she was talking to a Filipino. Anyone who was with a Filipino at that time, if it was a white woman, we all knew. It was that kind of a community. It was difficult growing up half. My mother's family wouldn't accept me. Later, my mother went with a Hungarian, and then an Irish guy, who was my stepfather. She was with him for more than fifty years.

So when it came to getting married to Albert, I was pretty much on the defensive about it, and I think that one of the reasons I got married was to prove I was as good as anybody else. Camille wasn't thrilled to death about it, but once we had our son Michael, she would become very defensive about it. "'Yeah she's Filipino. So what." That kind of thing.

I live up on Telegraph Hill now, and I look down at the building on Broadway, and that's the building where my mother met my father, at the Dimasalang dance hall. I've always found the whole racial aspect of it very curious. To be in the convent, I had to say I was Spanish and Italian, and I can remember my mother saying that. I was about five years old. My stepfather's family never knew I was Filipino. They told them I was Spanish.

It was because my stepfather was chief of police, though, that I got to work with the Navy at Hunter's Point, for special services and the Navy exchange. I took care of the books for both of them, at a time when there weren't many contracts. I was with the Navy for seven years.

Albert and I remained friendly. Even my mother and Albert's mother were close; they lived together at the end of their lives in a house in Brisbane. All our lives, there was never any animosity between Albert and I. We just went separate ways. We called him "Daddy." Daddy and Michael and I would meet for breakfast every Saturday morning, until Daddy got sick. And Michael did live with him for a little bit, more than twenty years ago. Sometimes, Michael will play the song "I Did It My Way" by Frank Sinatra, and I can't stand the song. But he says he thinks that the guys will be playing it in the bar, and that it reminds him of Daddy.

Mrs. Stuehler and her son, Al Flynn

We called him

DAD

As told by

JONI WALKER

Portrait by TONI ZERNIK, 2017

Joni's mother, Anna Flynn, tended bar at 7 Mile House for at least fifteen years. Like many girls in the 1950s, she married young, at eighteen. After divorcing her husband, she moved from Cupertino to San Francisco, stayed at the Geneva Hotel, and cocktailed at Castle Lanes, a bowling alley on Geneva. There, she met Al Flynn, and later got a second job at 7 Mile House. Joni met her future stepfather when she was ten years old, in 1967. She and her siblings would come down for the summer months; her sister Anna, whom bar regulars would call "Little Anna," moved in with Al and Big Anna in 1974. Soon, they were all calling him Dad, and even when Al and Anna divorced, everyone—Anna, her seven kids, grandkids, and Al—remained close, like family. When Al died, Big Anna was living with Little Anna; she had developed dementia and Alzheimer's. Whether Big Anna was aware of the enormity of the news of Al's passing, we'll never know.

Who would marry somebody with seven kids?! Yeah, he must've really loved my mom. We called him "Dad." He had tickets for many, many years for the San Francisco Giants, at Candlestick. I'd bring my friends over from Fremont to watch. When I got married, he would come out to Fremont for Thanksgiving and Christmas…he was so impressed about my family life. "I didn't know you had all this in you, Joni. You and your husband have a home!" he said. He bought us an antique dining table and our first washer and dryer.

Al was tall, very handsome. A gentleman always. Never belligerent, never drunk. His drink was a vodka and grapefruit juice, or a Bloody Mary. But he drank in moderation.

I can't say enough about my dad Al. When he started getting sick, I'd visit him at the hospital. I'd see him almost every week. And my mom and him—they were very good friends, and hung out just as much as when they were married.

Mrs. Stuehler and her son, Al Flynn

(Left) Al Flynn married Anna in Reno on December 5, 1970. "Who would marry someone with seven kids? Yeah, he must've really loved my mom," says Joni, Anna's daughter.

One Block Above the Cow Palace · 3 MINUTES FROM CANDLESTICK PARK

L&L Castle LANES

Open 24 Hours

1750 GENEVA AVENUE · SAN FRANCISCO · JUNIPER 6-9550

(Right) Al Flynn flanked by his stepdaughters, Toni and Joni, in the early 1990s. They all remained close, even when their mother, Anna and Al divorced. (Above) An old ad for Castle Lanes, where Big Anna worked as a cocktail waitress.

Toni, Al & Joni

(Left) Anna Flynn on Christmas in the 1980s. Behind her is daughter Sylvia. (Below) Al, Joni, and old friend Mark Moore.

(Left) Al, Joni, Benny and Little Anna (Anna Southwick) at the 7 Mile. (Below left) Joni, Anna, and Anna's best friend, Ginger Cotter. (Below) Anna's "Seven", as her kids were known in 1994 (from top to bottom): Marion, Mark, Toni, Anna, Joni, Sylvia, Michael.

This was the 7 Mile House that Camille and Al Flynn-era regulars were familiar with: no frills but homey, and always replete with memories and history.

Last of the

HORSEPLAYERS

As told by

BILL "THE GOOSE" LEGASSE

Portrait by TONI ZERNIK, 2017

Aside from old stories about the restaurant, the interviews revealed stories about bygone, halcyon days when things were purer, more vibrant—when places and people didn't need an Instragram filter to be more interesting, and when things didn't have to be instant to be gratifying. Bill "The Goose" Legasse, in his narration of his childhood in Pleasanton and bar-hopping days with Al Flynn, was one such source of these in-full-Technicolor-type tales. Listening to him was like listening to a travelogue of all the cool places in the 1960s and 1970s. He endeared himself to us more by making the effort to write his memories—some funny, some bittersweet—down in his neat block lettering. It was a reminder of how considerate people of his generation are, and how it doesn't hurt to regain a habit for preparing for things with an ample amount of care and conscientiousness, especially in a time when slapdash-ness and haste have become *de rigueur*.

graduated from Polytech in San Francisco in 1959. Two weeks after I graduated, I was upstairs at home, hanging out with my buddies, and my mother yells, "Bill! Get down here!" And my father's there, stretched across the table. He's purple and couldn't get his breath, and falls off the chair. I'm just a skinny kid. I grab him, we both go down on Bryant Street, and he ended up dying of a massive heart attack. I didn't know how to give artificial respiration. My mother phoned the San Francisco hospital, they sent the paramedics over, and they said, "Hey kid, he's gone." And I just graduated two weeks before. So my mother ended up going back to work in her late fifties. That's just some of the things that occur in life, I guess.

My father gave me many good memories going to the fairs in Pleasanton. If you have the time, even if it's changed pretty much, you should go. Flower shows, cart shows, cotton candy, horse racing—it's always a fun time. I always look forward to it. I've been going since I was a child. The fairs had just started up after World War II. My uncles had come back from New Guinea, the Philippines, and people were rebuilding their lives, getting married. It was a different time.

My father would bring me up there even if I was too young, but we would play the horses.

THAT'S WHERE I MET A BUNCH OF PEOPLE—I MET **AL** BEFORE HE MARRIED **ANNA,** IN AROUND 1969. TALL, QUIET GUY. I MET A GUY NAMED **KENNY OWENS, NARDI, BOBBY RIGGS,** AND **SOME OLDER GUYS.** WE ENDED UP DOING THE SAME THING AGAIN—**RACETRACKS.**

He would pick this one, that one, and put down two dollars for me. My parents also liked to play poker and we used to have house poker games. Eventually I started playing poker at sixteen years old with adults—I sat with them and ended up winning their paychecks—and I was also lucky with the horses.

I was always raised around older people. They'd talk about philosophy and psychology—so I'd sit around and listen. I wasn't like my little friend Johnny down the block; I was really learning something. I hung around adults and I learned adult ways. I was an adult by the time I was sixteen years old.

My aunts, uncles, they enjoyed going to Reno or Tahoe. They used to drive up there in the old 1940s cars, nobody ever had a new car. I'd walk through town. And then I introduced my friends whom I went to junior high with to the fair. We were under-aged, but we looked older, we acted older, so we always got tickets to play the horses. They could've checked our I.D. but...they didn't. Then one by one, the girls got pregnant and started getting married. Our youngest one was sixteen years old and in junior high.

I was twenty-three when I got drafted. I was one of the oldest guys in the barracks. I never thought they'd get me. I was drafted into the service just before Vietnam in '63, and I spent two years in Fort Lewis, Washington. By the time I got out, my friends and I didn't go out much anymore. They had families to raise, so I was a little lost. I was by myself, and one of the guys who was in my group. they used to call him Mousy—he introduced me to a group of people down the Mission and 24th Street. That's where I met a bunch of people—I met Al before he married Anna, in around 1969. Tall, quiet guy. I met a guy named Kenny Owens, Nardi, Bobby Riggs, and some older guys. We ended up doing the same thing again—racetracks. No poker for me anymore, I was over the poker fad. Nardi,

THE WHOLE THRUST OF THE THING WAS: **WE ALL LIKED TO HAVE A GOOD TIME. "I'LL SEE YOU AT THE SEVEN."**

One of the familiar faces in 7 Mile was Jebbie, an old bartender.

Kenny Owens, Larry Morales—they were all in the Korean War, too.

Life then was exciting. You got people asking, "Hey what are you doing next weekend?" "Okay, we'll all meet here—wanna go to the Roaring '20s or the Red Garter or the piano bars?" We'd take a car up to Luke's Club, right across a funeral home, and we all knew each other there. Then we'd go down to the Diamond Club which was on Harrison and 24th.

We'd go to Pop's Corner and there was Roosevelt Creamery across the street, and we'd have milk shakes and sodas. Further down, there was Jack's Club. We'd go to dinners—Capp's Corner in North Beach, Alfred's Steakhouse. Everybody knew everybody.

Then Al married Anna. We'd go down visit her at the 16 Mile House where she was a waitress. Anna also bartended at the Waterfront before Al married her. They used to go to The Green Lantern.

Eventually, some of the guys we knew who were in the Korean War died, and there was hardly anyone in San Francisco who liked to play the horses. So Bobby Riggs and Nardi moved up to Brisbane, so I moved up too because there was no one my age in San Francisco anymore.

Chico used to work hamburgers here. There was a guy working here named Jebbie. There was Jerry the electrician; now he's at The Topper quite a lot. A guy named Richie Morrey, who owned The Green Lantern. They all went to Bertolucci's. A guy named Flavio was the *maître d'* there.

*The Topper is located in South City. It opened in 1941 and is still operated by the
Cattaneo family. Benny Hernandez moved there after I purchased 7 Mile House
in 2004. At 88 years old, Benny still tends bar five times a week.*

The whole thrust of the thing was: we all liked to have a good time. "I'll see you at the Seven."

There was an old man. Cowboy Mike, we used to call him. Short guy. He wore a cowboy hat, and he was a member of the American Horsemen's Association. They used to ride in the Grand National and all the parades in San Francisco. Cowboy Mike was in the movies with John Wayne, he played the part of the Indian, naturally. One of many stories about Cowboy Mike is that he had to bring Nardi down to the eye doctor for an operation of some sort. He parks across the street—now Mike can't see worth a darn—Nardi's got the dark glasses on, and we're looking out the door. We see Mike crossing Bayshore, right there in the middle of the street coming right towards here. "Now here's the blind leading the blind," we say. "Oh, nooo…." Two blind people leading each other across the traffic and we're looking out and just waiting for something to happen.

Nardi, meanwhile, he liked to drink a lot. He used to come here, get stuff to go, and put it on the roof of his car. He would drink a lot and forget about the food and it would blow away. He did this all the time. It was, "here we go again." Whoop! Food all over the place. Nardi would walk from the 7 or any place—Eagle's Club, the 23 Club, The Brisbane Inn—and there's a twenty dollar

Bill Legasse with brothers Danny and Leo Arnelis on Al Flynn's last day as 7 Mile owner. Bill still shows up occasionally, and still attends the Pleasanton fairs every year.

bill here, ten dollar bill there. Somebody would say, "Has Nardi been here?" He'd stuff money in his pocket and it would fall out. But somebody always picked it up and gave it back to him.

Here's one more story: Nardi's loaded as usual, and he's driving from here back to Brisbane, and he's very slow. He's got a few of the guys in the car, and everybody's passing him by. He says, "Geez they all know me, they're all waving at me!" They're all beeping their horns but they aren't waving at him—they're giving him the finger: "Move!" And Nardi's waving back, thinking they're all his friends.

Us regulars, we'd come down on weekends, watch the baseball game. We liked sports, we liked to eat. 7 Mile was always a very friendly place. After the guys, I used to come here with a lady named Evelyn. That was twelve years ago; we came down here for the lunches. We lived together for twenty years. We loved to take trips, cruises. She was a lovely woman.

The 7 was like an old home. Everyone knew each other. For fifty years, I knew them. But all have passed. Of the older crew of the horseplayers, I'm the only one that's left.

Mrs. Stuehler and her son, Al Flynn

Lessons from my

FATHER

As told by

RON LEE MOORE

Portrait by TONI ZERNIK, 2017

One of the more emotional conversations I had during the making of this book was with Ron Lee Moore, who we christened "The Tattoo Guy" on account of his 7 Mile House tattoo. His tattoo is more than a sentimental tribute to a bar—it's an homage to his father. Kenneth Moore made an indelible mark (no pun intended) on his kids for his hardworking ways and strong principles—a true "maestro" for steering his family from the humblest beginnings and instilling in them rock solid family values. The way Ron describes his father is exactly the way I want my children to see me. "I'm sure they do," Ron reassured me. "You have so much strength, and you show them the strength that you have, by your daily doing." I believe onion-cutting ninjas entered the room as the interview drew to a close.

y dad's name was Kenneth Moore, and he was a maestro at what he did.

He didn't do anything grand. My dad wasn't famous, but how he lived his life enriched my brother and I so much. His legacy to us started even while we were little—and even if he's passed on from this world, we feel his presence with us.

My father started bartending here at 7 Mile when I was six years old. He bartended here from around 1967 to 1970. This was his second job—he used to work in Cargill around this area, which I think was some kind of food factory. After his shift there, he'd come here. The owner, Camille, probably saw something in him, so she offered him a job.

I was too young to understand finances, but what I know is that in the early Sixties, my dad had just gotten out of the service. He had met my mother while he was still in it. He would hitchhike from San Diego to here to see her. For extra cash, he would donate blood for money, and I'm guessing he was offered extra because he had a rare blood type, as well.

When my parents got married and had me and my brother, we lived in the Excelsior District. My mother went to beautician school while my father held down his two jobs in Cargill and 7 Mile House. After school, my brother and I would walk here and watch our father work. Camille, in turn, would keep an eye on us. She

CAMILLE WOULD TAKE CARE OF MY BROTHER AND I. WE WOULD SIT AT THE BAR OVER THERE AND SHE'D **KEEP AN EYE** ON US TWO MISCHIEVOUS BOYS AND GIVE US **SARSAPARILLA** AND **SHIRLEY TEMPLES.**

Ron and his brother, also named Kenneth, like to reminisce about their childhood years spent watching their father work in 7 Mile. This photo was taken in April 1966. (Opposite page) A leather cup and set of dice used in playing Liar's Dice—another gem I found while cleaning up 7 Mile's old cabinets and drawers.

took care of my brother and I like we were her own kids. We would sit at the bar over there and she'd give us sarsaparilla and Shirley Temples. I was always comfortable here. Camille was always very nice.

After our father's shift, he'd play pool with some of the customers. I remember them playing pool for beer, and my father would have drinks lined up at the bar—whether they were for him or for another player, I don't know. It was all very fascinating for me as a young boy. While some played pool, other men played Liar's Dice at the bar. They'd shake the cup and slam it down and it looked like they were all having a good time. Everyone knew each other.

My father was a firm, almost exacting, man. But he exercised it in a way that people grew to respect, not resent, him. Seeing people respond to him that way was almost magical for my brother and I. The way he talked to them, like he was touching something inside them that made them laugh, or say a kind, funny thing, or defer to him in a certain way; the way he moved behind the bar, quickly and efficiently, but never losing his cool. It was extra magical because we saw it happening in a place full of adults, and we were literally in the middle of it all, the busiest part of

"I'm sixty-five percent tattooed. My father, when he was alive, would look at me and go: 'What have you done?' So I have another tattoo, an eagle, so I bring my father with me wherever I go."

the business. You'd think we'd be treated like furniture, but we were just as accepted and made welcome. It was very unusual.

People might say a bar isn't the best environment to bring your kids. It may have been an *unusual* environment, but it wasn't a *bad* environment. Seeing my father work, keeping everything under control, and keeping everyone happy was a learning process for me and my brother. As I grew older, I began to understand how difficult this might have been for him. But he took this bartending job because he was trying to be the best provider, and made us stay with him because whatever time he could have with us, he'd take it. No matter what the circumstance. He was really trying to be a great father and provider.

Right before I turned ten, my father began as a street sweeper in the San Francisco Water Department. Things changed for us after that. My parents got to purchase a home; our lives kind of changed for the better. But my father worked just as hard—he wouldn't leave work, even when he got sick. And he continued to come to 7 Mile a few days in the evenings after work, and mostly on weekends too. 7 Mile didn't change throughout the years—there was still a lot of camaraderie, and it was a warm, full place. Not congested, but full enough to make it inviting. My father was also an avid wrestling fan, so we would go to the Cow Palace, and after, we would come here. 7 Mile continued to be a part of our family.

My father passed away very young due to throat cancer. He was only fifty. Though me and my brother

Mrs. Stuehler and her son, Al Flynn

Ron's father, sister, and brother. His father was toughest on the younger Kenneth, but Ron could see that he was being extra hard because he was building him up as the head of the family in case anything untoward happened. He was building *all* of them up.

were both close to my father, my brother was closer and took the brunt of his expectations, maybe because he was the oldest boy. They worked together for twelve years in the Water Department in Sonoma, so they were workmates, as well as father and son, and their relationship was loving as well as rigorous, like a general passing on the baton. My father took his role very seriously; as the leader of the family, he was devoted to us in all aspects. He wanted to be sure we were ready for life. At work, he never took any time off. They had to retire him due to his illness. But he left my mom—the woman he adored and hitchhiked for just so he could see her on furlough—very well-to-do.

This was the kind of man whose shoes my brother was expected to fill. My father kept telling him, "If anything happens, you're going to take over this family, so you better be ready,

Kenneth Moore, Ron's father and hero. He showed what grace, integrity, and leadership was by his work ethic and devotion to his family.

emotionally, physically." It was tough. But I understood what my father was putting him through when he was doing it. It built my brother up; it built all of us up.

I stopped coming to 7 Mile as an adult when I got into the service. Then I moved to Washington state for about twenty-two years. But every time I came home to California for whatever reason, I would always try to stop by here, just to say hello to the memory of my father. When I got out of the service, I came here for a drink with my friends. And then when I lived in South City from 1985 till 1992, I would come in 7 Mile once or twice a year or so, just for a drink and be here, in the environment and reminisce. When my brother moved to Newark, and when we would go to visit my grandmother, there wasn't a time when we wouldn't be passing by here. He wouldn't go on the freeway, he'd get off and go to Bayshore to see this place. This is where it started. This is where my brother and I first learned our most valuable lessons in life.

My father's most enduring words to us were: "This is what you're going to do, and this is how you're going to do it, and you're going to do the best you can." That was the attitude he gave us. To watch him at the bar—and throughout life, for that matter—was a splendid sight. Not only was he teaching—he was showing, and doing. We weren't just hanging around at the bar, we were learning something every minute. I guess I got this 7 Mile tattoo because of what it symbolizes: the place, and how my father helped me get through and get what I got out of this life. I got it because wanted to thank him for that.

I've had this tattoo for fifteen years now. I was in Washington when I got it. I have another one that links me to my dad. My father, being in the Navy, always wanted an eagle all the way across his chest but he never got it. I, being the crazy one I guess, I'm sixty-five percent tattooed. My father, when he was alive, would look at me and go, "What in the hell have you done?" So I have another tattoo, an eagle. Now I can bring my father with me wherever I go.

My brother and I talk about this place quite a bit. We talked about Camille the other day, probably a week and a half ago, and we started talking just about how my dad was, how everybody liked him here. The man that he was. Those early years taught me to get after what I was getting after, and now even I tell my kids, "Get after what you're getting after in life. The world will beat you up, but you stay focused on life, on what you're getting at." That's a birthright born right here in 7 Mile. This place brings back a lot of the past with my father, but it's all good. I'm a man of memories, and I can still feel my father's presence in the memories I make today.

'THE RYKOFF BAR'

A h, the Seventies.

Watergate. The Indochina War. The Equal Rights Amendment. These were a few of the major issues that engrossed the nation during that decade.

Over in Brisbane, California, though, people—drivers, warehousemen, unionists—were preoccupied with less pressing matters. To wear a seatbelt or not? To hire a stripper to come to the warehouse for a friend's birthday, or just get a cake, or both? What to wear—or not wear—to the annual Exotic Erotic Ball, the biggest public adult-themed festival in the world held nearby at the Cow Palace? Decisions, decisions.

Not to say these folks weren't one with the rest of the country. If anything, they knew its pulse and its most intimate sentiments—because they were at the very heart of it. Among them were men who served the U.S., men who were to be teachers and influencers of young minds, men who were going to contribute healthily to the country's economy one day.

It just so happened that most of them worked at S.E. Rykoff & Co., a wholesale grocer that serviced restaurants, hotels and other institutions from warehouses and truck fleets across the U.S.; were part of the Teamsters, a powerful North American union founded in 1903; and that many of them convened in a little dive called the 7 Mile House.

John Walsh (left), who became a regular in 1973 after he left the Navy and joined S.E. Rykoff as a driver. (Opposite) Regulars from Rykoff in 1983. On the back, it says: John E. Walsh, Bob Pagan, Ron Foss, Frank Borelli, Joe Jarvera, Guiedo (last name unknown), John Colter.

"It was our home away from home," says Michael Tomola, who joined Rykoff in 1977, when he was only twenty-one. To his recollection, "the guys from ILWU (International Longshore and Warehouse Union) came during the daytime. Teamsters came around 8 or 9 p.m. Rykoff guys." No matter what union they belonged to, coming to 7 Mile was a sort of initiation. "It was a pretty inclusive group. Some of the more senior people would invite you over and you had a sort of orientation period, so to speak."

John Walsh, who had just gotten out from the Navy after twenty-two years of service was already thirty-seven years old when he started driving for Rykoff. "Hell, I had to do something!" He got the job in 1973, and stayed for the next twenty-five years.

"7 Mile became a habit," John continues. "After driving for a day, I'd stop by for a quick tipple. They had a phone booth inside. I used to call my wife from there. I'd be there an hour and I'd call her and say I just got in," he says with a laugh. "Then she'd say, 'don't stay too long.' She was so sweet. She knew."

Teamsters weren't the only types drawn to 7 Mile. During circus season at the Cow Palace, "a strange group of people would come down," Michael muses. "Strange, but nice." Mitch Conliffe, another Teamster who worked at Rykoff from 1979 to 1983, remembers seeing a fellow with a chandelier in his car—right where the dome light was supposed to be.

Whoever it was—activist or stripper, gambler or ex-serviceman, as long as you weren't an asshole, or a child molester like John Anthony Castellanos, who stopped by the bar for drinks before assaulting a nine-year-old girl along Bayshore Boulevard in 1987—7 Mile welcomed them all. "It was like a United Nations meeting in there," says Michael. "Filipino, Tongan, black, Hispanic. We all got along. And that was what was cool about it."

BARTENDERS
DO IT BETTER

7 Mile House has had some pretty legendary bartenders. Most often mentioned but impossible to get ahold of—unless we resorted to séances and black magic—were Jebbie Alfonso and Chico. Jebbie Alfonso was a tall, balding old man with crooked teeth and a funny titter, who worked there for seventeen years, "a good guy who fell off the wagon" and eventually ended up homeless. Chico, who most thought was Samoan, was really Puerto Rican, and tended bar for ten years. He was a former boxer with "Popeye arms," who liked to smoke his weed, was called "Dr. Chico," and who many describe as very low-key and gentle mannered. In lieu of Al cashing checks, he was the Rykoff guys' human ATM. "When we would run out of the money in the middle of the week, we'd go to Chico and say we need a hundred bucks to get through Friday. He would write a Post-It note, write your name, and he stick it above the mirror behind the bar. No interest, all honor system. You always paid back, and he remembered all this," shares ex-Rykoff warehouseman Michael Tomola.

There were a few we did get to know, though, either through their relatives and face-to-face. All prove that bartenders are a whipsmart, exciting lot.

ANNA FLYNN *knew how to get creative when it came to getting customers to let go of their cash. "If it was your birthday," Joni says, "You'd have to roll up a dollar and throw it behind the back bar. I've sat down and watched money fly over that bar. If ever that back bar comes down, that's got some money behind it. Or if she was going for a vacation, she'd have a separate tip jar and make people put tips in both jars."*

RICHARD HUERTAS *started hanging around the bar when he was sixteen or seventeen—not yet old enough to drive, but his dad Emilio would always ask him to be his designated driver. Richard was always eager to drop by. "It was fun; I knew all of them, and they knew me," he says, in his gruff voice and rapid staccato. His first bartending gig was at the Pinch Hit bar, and then was asked by Camille if he wanted to help out his Uncle Chico, who was getting old and slowing down. That was around 1979, when he was already twenty-two years old. Though he didn't last long and only worked the weekends, he always made sure to check on Uncle Chico. One rare, tension-filled night, he had to step in during a fight—not to lend muscle to his ex-boxer uncle, but to restrain him. "Eh, but he punched the guy anyway," Richard says, laughing. "So I punched the other guy too and the third ran out." He broke his hand in that fight—you can see how it's still a little crooked today. All for the love of Uncle Chico and keeping the peace at 7 Mile.*

JONI WALKER *may have been a drinker—here she is with Benny, enjoying her favorite combo: a Jose Cuervo tequila and Budweiser—but she always knew how to hold her liquor. She began waitressing, and then bartending, at the 7 Mile in 1985 after a devastating divorce. She bartended in the Diamond Club and Babes Tower, as well. "You become sort of a professional drinker if people are buying you drinks," she says of the job. In those days, it was still legal to drink behind the bar, which made it more tempting. "But even so, you have to stay busy and polite and respectful. If you're conscientious and not bullshitting with one person, and you're making sure you know what's going on, everybody's happy, even if it's three-deep. It was fun and all the guys were very respectful." She also never allowed her work to interfere with her time with her kids. "The bar scene is not what you want to give your kids. If you allow yourself to get impaired, you forget about your responsibilities and all you want to do is have fun."*

LUNCH, BEERS, COMING UP!

Before the general populace proved that it couldn't be trusted with certain liberties, and that certain restrictions had to be imposed on almost everything that made life fun and quirky and, well, just a little bit risky, it was accepted that people drank on the job. In moderation, of course, but they were allowed to squeeze in a nip or two midday.

PG&E was one company that gave its employees this freedom. In fact, it even had its own club house on the premises, outfitted with a full bar. For a short period in the 1980s, it was possible to get alcohol through a window at 7 Mile. The place's liquor license allowed it to sell six packs and alcohol to go, and this is what people from PG&E would do. It helped that the lots were adjacent to each other, and there was a convenient window. "I can't imagine doing that now," a PG&E old timer says. "Those were very different, more lenient times."

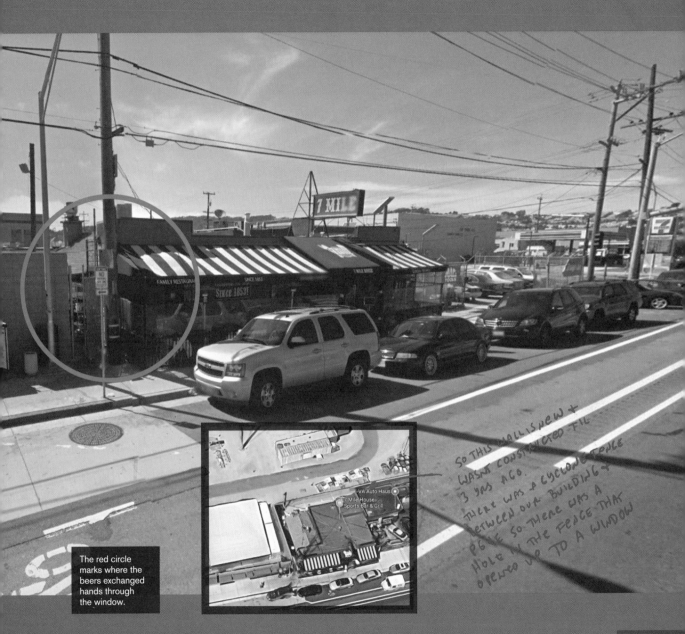

7 MILE

The red circle marks where the beers exchanged hands through the window.

So this mall is new + wasn't constructed til 3 yrs ago. There was a cyclone fence between our building + 7 mile so there was a hole in the fence that opened up to a window

147

DORIS AND THE 7 MILE BURGER

'Y ou haven't even nailed it," Joni Walker teases me as I bring up the renowned 7 Mile Burger by a woman named Doris (no matter how hard we tried, we could not trace her or anyone who might have known her outside the restaurant). Al brought in Doris from neighboring Darby Dan's where she made sandwiches, to open the kitchen in the 1980s, and let her have complete autonomy. Food and drinks were ordered and billed separately.

Aside from burgers, she also served tacos, enchiladas, a soup of the day made from scratch, and "great breakfasts," according to Joni. There were daily specials, too—there was a Meatloaf Day, Chicken Day, and so on. Orders were only up to 3 p.m. The following ingredients are what the regulars could remember; and we can only guess what the exact measurements were. If anyone out there has the wherewithal to do some experimentation, invite us over and let us have a bite!

BUNS:
Your way—a regular bun or Hoagie roll, both toasted

PATTY:
Half-pound, your way—round or long; single or double

TOPPINGS:
Avocado
Tomatoes in thick slices
Raw onions in thick slices
Cheese
Mayonnaise
Lettuce
Bacon

SIDES:
Salsa
Thick-cut fries

Recreated and photographed by
TONI ZERNIK, 2017

MANNY'S
MENU

After Doris left, Mexican chef Manuel "Manny" Herrera took over the 7 Mile kitchen.

A former CPA who worked for the Bank of Mexico, Manny barely knew any English when he came to California in 1955. He thought he would be shipped out to service, but was kept in the reserves. He started to learn the restaurant trade when he worked in his first restaurant in North Beach as a dishwasher. "I knew how to cook," he explains, "my father had a couple of restaurants. But I had to start somewhere."

Eventually, Manny got a job at Circle Star. From what we understand, it was a theater restaurant that also allowed their chefs to go on tours with big stars. He cooked for the likes of Frank Sinatra, Tom Jones, and Julio Iglesias. But he got tired of all the traveling. He mentioned it to Benny Hernandez—his drinking partner over at 7 Mile House—and Benny mentioned it to Camille. "That's how it started," Manny says, his voice placid, and accent still thick.

Manny's domain was to be what we now call the semi-private dining room. "There were no tablecloths, no curtains, no nothing," he recalls. With Benny's help, he redid the walls with wallpaper in green and white flowers, and decked the tables with tablecloths with red flowers. Like Doris, they opened only for breakfast and lunch.

The items he made were inexpensive, and not difficult to cook. A sampling of Manny's menu would be:

SANDWICHES
Grilled cheese
Ham
Egg
Steak

PASTA
Scallopini
Clams in white sauce ("If they wanted it red, all I have to do is put marinara sauce. If white, I use white wine, but not too much olive oil because it kills the flavor.")

ITALIAN
Chicken parmigiana
Chicken cacciatorre

The bestseller was still the 7 Mile Burger. Manny kept Doris' version (including the choice of bread and shape of patty) except for a few tweaks: Wheat bread was made available
French bread took the place of a hoagie roll
Grilled onions
Sauteed mushrooms
Garlic oil

Manny's kitchen grew so successful that his wife and daughter came in to help. In his last few months, he had to hire a dishwasher because it got too busy. When Benny left in 2004, he packed up as well. Truly, some good things never last. Now retired, Manny walks every morning to the Garden Club in South City where he hangs out and helps the bartender prep limes and lemons.

Recreated and photographed by TONI ZERNIK, 2017

BENNY'S BLOODY MARY

Benny Hernandez—of all people—refused to go on the record for this book. All we have that can be directly attributed to him is this quote: "I look young because I drink a lot."

A former butcher, Benny started bartending in 7 Mile in 1982. Disputably 7 Mile's most popular bartender, he's amassed such a loyal following that all of 7 Mile's old regulars followed him to The Topper in South San Francisco, where he began bartending when I took over in 2004. At eighty-eight years old, Benny is still the bartender to beat—he remembers what you like to drink, how you like it, and is equal parts sweet-smart-snarky. And secretive. We're lucky he even agreed to have his photo taken, and that he shared with us the ingredients of his famous Bloody Mary. Sorry, portions not included. You have to figure that out for yourself.

WHAT'S IN IT:
Salt
Pepper
Fresh horseradish
Vodka
Tabasco Bloody Mary Mix
Worcestershire sauce

TONI ZERNIK, 2017

TUMBLEWEED

Photo by TONI ZERNIK, 2017

A CLASSIC DIVE GETS A MAKEOVER; RUNNING THE BUSINESS WITH HEART; AND MAKING THE NOW OUT OF NOTHING (2004 – PRESENT)

ery few things intimidate me. I don't say that to sound brave or strong—on the contrary, people will say I'm even foolhardy, and plunge into things that I know very little about. Here's why I do them: I figure, if God put these things in front of me, they're something he wants me to try out. I just have to find a way how.

But 7 Mile House intimidated me. Before my ex-husband and I decided to take over, I never stepped into the place. That's something I regret, but it was only open for lunch Mondays to Fridays, and I was tied down to my day job at Citigate Cunningham. I think I just went in once or twice to get a soda, and it was really dark, and looked pretty unwelcoming.

All the bars I had been to before, especially in the Philippines, were spanking new and polished. Even the clubs I played in as a drummer back home were, if not swanky, located in upscale districts. The concept of the American dive was new to me—those well-worn places where the guests and the conversation and the inside jokes were part of the patina, where people went to not just because of

Old regulars applaud Al Flynn on his last day. This was a bittersweet day for us all. I was stepping in as new steward of the 7—a newbie, an "outsider" who saw these people as new friends, full of optimism for the next chapter of 7 Mile. For the old customers, it was a celebration of decades of camara- derie—but a realization that those memories had to make way for new ones.

the drinks and food, but the camaraderie. But we are prone to fear what we don't understand. Now, I realize, dives are much more comfortable. Dives allow you to be just *you*. Nobody really cares about who you are and why you came in.

At that time, it also seemed nobody wanted 7 Mile House—or at least, on the conditions on which it was being given up. The landlords, which included my former in-laws since they went into business with the Agustins, wanted to continue to rent out the space on a month-to-month basis, and there were no takers on the lease. Who in their right mind would agree to those terms? The restaurant was going to close, and with it, a hundred years' worth of history and memories.

They say things happen for a reason, that 7 Mile House came my way because I have the moxie and Disneyland attitude—la-la-la, the sun is shining and all is hopeful and well—that it needed for a fresh life. This included doing crazy things like standing in the middle of Bayshore, on that island in the center of the street, to give people fliers while they were in their cars. Or going house-to-house in San Francisco and Brisbane, and putting fliers in their mailboxes, just to build an audience. Or sitting with one customer for five hours until it was legally time to kick her out, even if my tentative, over-polite Filipino instincts railed against it. Or, on Benny's last day at 7 Mile House,

Al is flanked by his two loyal bartenders, Benny Hernandez and Allan;
(right) the ceremonial handing over of 7 Mile House's keys.

creating fliers and telling everyone, "This is your 7 Mile House, you're welcome to come back." I gave those fliers to *everyone*! I wanted to make people feel that this would still be their place. But hardly anyone came back. I started from scratch. I started from nothing.

I think it also came my way because of a pivotal moment in my family: My mom and dad were splitting up. My perfect, beautiful family was in turmoil. I didn't know what to feel or who to side

Al Flynn and his 7 Mile House family. Everyone came out to play. But it would take years before the old regulars came back to check out the new 7 Mile House. Among them, only Tony Ragusin (second from right, in dark gray hoodie), has consistently showed up to this day.

with—I just felt that I was drowning alongside my mom in this new reality that she was up against, and I offered her this opportunity. "This is your chance to have a new life," I told her. "Mom, I'm not going to do this without you." And she said okay. So I went to bartending school in San Francisco. We bought the restaurant in October 2004 and formally launched in February 2005. We tried opening up for service here and there—half-hearted attempts at testing the waters. We went back to the Philippines during these lapses because my ex-husband said we'd better go home since we figured wouldn't have a chance anymore after that. The next time I would be back was 2016.

While we were gone, my former cousins-in-law, *Kuya* Jimmy ("kuya" means older brother in Filipino; a form of respect that we use when addressing older males) and his wife, *Ate* Lory, were renovating by themselves ("ate" means older sister). When I came back, we did the floors, took out the paintings behind the bar, changed the kitchen counter, slapped plywood on the white and green walls. The walls in the main bar were half plaster, half wood, so we covered the plaster part with wood.

My selfless, loving family taking a break from our DIY renovation days, in late 2004. That's (from left) my former father-in-law Gene Villacarlos, *Kuya* Jimmy, my former sister-in-law's husband John Mack, and *Ate* Lory.

I didn't really do much re-design, just sprucing up. My purpose was not to change anything, but to leave things as is. Just brighter, cleaner, more inviting. It was really the outside that I was more concerned about—first it was yellow, then it became red, then brown. I tried different colors, but it was the construction of the sidewalk by the Brisbane local government and the patio that helped out a lot.

We had four things on the menu: hamburger, *lumpia* (Filipino egg rolls), wings, and *sisig* (diced pork cheeks, pork meat, some liver, barbequed and chopped, spiced up and served on a sizzling plate topped with raw egg). The kitchen wasn't open yet and mom was doing some experimentation. One failure was the hamburger. In the Philippines, we usually put a lot of stuff in it—carrots, garlic, even pork and all that. We tried different flavors before we realized how naive we were—why were we trying to mess with the flavor of the meat? Doris and Manny would have hung their heads in shame. Our *sisig*, meanwhile, was outsourced in those days. I used to buy it in Alameda—only one tray every few days because we didn't have a lot of customers, and we were open only on the weekends for lunch and dinner.

After a few days, mom quit as our cook (but stayed on as a server). She couldn't take the

(Top left and right) The old kitchen counter, before and after. (Below left) A longer view of what the semi-private dining area looked like. (Below right) The same area now. We dug up three layers of linoleum so we could re-do the floors.

Our now-famous lumpia *(left) and* sisig *with rice (right), now all cooked in-house.*

pressure of a commercial kitchen. My ex-husband used to say: "Mom, food's taking too long! Customers have been waiting for a long time!" It was a classic case of successful home cook realizing the enormity of responsibility that comes with a trade kitchen. Without a cook and not knowing to whom to turn, I confessed to a client at my corporate job what was going on in my other life. She was Renee Reyes, daughter of George Reyes of Old Clam House fame. Probably sensing my utter need, she offered to set up a meeting for me and her dad. So one day, she brought him in, and he fell in love with the place because it reminded him of how the Old Clam House was back in the day. We talked and I admitted I couldn't pay him his consultancy fee, but we reached an agreement to pay him what I could. *Tito* (or Uncle) George not only ended up doing most of the cooking at this point—he didn't

THE KITCHEN WASN'T OPEN YET AND **MOM** WAS **DOING SOME EXPERIMENTATION.** ONE FAILURE WAS THE **HAMBURGER.** IN THE **PHILIPPINES**, WE USUALLY PUT A LOT OF STUFF IN IT—**CARROTS, GARLIC, PORK** AND ALL THAT. WE TRIED DIFFERENT FLAVORS BEFORE WE REALIZED **HOW NAIVE WE WERE.**

My mentor, George Reyes of Old Clam House fame. He trained my kitchen staff and brought in customers. I don't know what I would've done without his guidance and advice.

The many facades of 7 Mile. I had to try different colors and combinations before I got the right formula of making it still look "old" but inviting. The sidewalk installed by the city of Brisbane helped immensely.

have to, but he's just such a kind soul—he also became a mentor to me.

Soon after, I left Citigate. I felt it was just wrong, thinking about my business while at work. My dad told me I wasn't being fair to my employer, and he was right—I couldn't do it. So I quit. Financially, that might not have been the wisest thing to do at the time. I had lost one income stream (and I learned that they started laying off people two months later—I could've gotten a severance package, damn!), and 7 Mile wasn't bringing in the same money to replace that. But my ex had a

Eventually, we put in a patio area. This made the place look more inviting, and made it possible for our guests to bring their dogs along.

good job, and I think people thought we were better off than we really were. One time, a person told me, "Hey you're the owner of 7 Mile, how much do you bring in for lunch—a thousand?" "Uh, no... we do three hundred a day." We were happy if we made five hundred dollars a day!

Who was nice enough to give us that three hundred every day? Post office people—they were nearby so they would come and hang out, and I'd hang out and drink with them, too. The biotech companies around the area—I was thankful for them. If anyone came from the old 7 Mile, it was once every six months. My customers were mostly in-laws, their friends, or relatives. *Tito* George also brought in a lot of customers from the Old Clam House, but it wasn't consistent, and other than that, hardly anyone was coming.

They say that eighty or ninety percent of restaurants here in the Bay Area fail within two years. It's hard, there's too much competition, too much money is invested, and the business fails. My formula is: don't spend what you don't have. We were very, very careful with our expenses. I didn't put any money in after our initial layout of seventy thousand. This amount was gotten from refinancing our home, not our savings, and we were so prudent that we were able to stretch it a long way. We used it to purchase our business and alcohol license, inventory, renovations, and some

Customers used to hold barbeques and drink beer outside the building. This led me to foolishly believe we'd be let off by the local authorities when we started doing it, as well. I was mistaken, and received at least four warnings.

capital, including salaries, to get us up and running. Every penny was put to good, justifiable use.

Aside from the location and lack of curb appeal, I was up against 7 Mile's reputation. Perceptions are very hard to change, especially when your place had been raided by the FBI in full light of day. Some people felt that bars brought on nothing but trouble for the community, and I understood, as that's what their experience was.

The police bore down on us for seemingly infinitesimal issues. First, we were cited for having guests and half a bottle of beer on the bar at two-thirty in the morning. It was our soft opening night in January 2005, the first time we started charging our guests. Three police cars came by, took photos and everything. I asked the officer if he could give us some leniency as it was our first day, and as my interpretation of the law — wrong as it was — was that I could serve alcohol anytime before 2 a.m. and people could hang around to finish their drinks after that. He said, "You should've told me that earlier. I already wrote the ticket." San Mateo Court dismissed the case. They didn't think it was serious enough to merit a punishment.

Second, we were also warned four or five times for drinking outside — which I thought was something the Brisbane community, or police force at least, had already grown accustomed to, considering all the old photos I've seen of people holding barbeques and drinking out front.

The sergeant started giving us warnings and finally, I hired a security guard to come in on the weekends to make sure people didn't drink on the sidewalk. But right before the guard started, the same sergeant cited us for having several bottles outside. I had to hire a lawyer to contest that. But the court deemed it an infraction instead of a misdemeanor.

In the same year, we were shut down one time for various reasons. The police cut the party early, and everyone was made to go home. I still feel a twitch around my heart when I remember that night. I needed that money. I needed that money to survive. Nobody knew our story. Nobody bothered to get to know me and the people who worked at 7 Mile. They didn't know that we were just a family with good intentions, that we didn't want to cause trouble or to bother anyone.

ASIDE FROM THE LOCATION AND **LACK OF CURB APPEAL**, I WAS UP AGAINST 7 MILE'S REPUTATION. PERCEPTIONS ARE VERY HARD TO CHANGE, ESPECIALLY WHEN YOU'VE BEEN **RAIDED BY THE FBI** IN THE LIGHT OF DAY.

This is the inventory Benny passed onto me. If only people realized how humbly we started—especially those who thought we meant to break laws. We were just a small operation—a family!—wanting to give other well-meaning folk steady jobs. We just wanted to make people happy, we weren't out to make trouble.

VODKA		BRANDY			
WELL VODKA	9.2	A.R MORROW	.7	COURVOISIER	1.2
SMIRNOFF	3.6	IIII PLUS	1	VERMOUTH	
IIII PLUS	2	KORBEL	1.8	DRY	1.5
ABSOLUTE	1.5	CHRIS BROTHER	2.3	VERMOUTH	
KETEL ONE	2	SCOTCH		SWEET	1.5
STOLI	2	WELL SCOTCH	2.4		
SKYY	2	J.B	1.8	BUD	
BOURBON		CUTTY SARK	.9	BUD LITE	
KESSLER	2	TEQUILA		BUD CAN	
IIII PLUS	1	WELL TEQUILA	.9	MILLER LITE	
JACK DANIELS	2.1	CUERVO GOLD	1.9	MILLER HIGH LITE	
V.O.	2.7	TRES GENERACION	1.9	COORS	
IIII PLUS	1	CAZADORES	1	COORS LITE	
7 AND 7	1.4	FERNET	1.6	SHORT BUD	
IIII PLUS	1	CAMPARI	1.8	MICHELOB ULTRA	
C.C.	2.8	ANISETTE	.9	M.G.D.	
EARLY TIMES	1.8	CREME THE MENTHE	1.6	CORONA	
JIM BEAM	2	GREEN IIII	1	GUINNESS	
OLD CROW	.8	SCHNAPPS	.8	KEG	
GIN		KAHLUA	1.7	HEINEKEN	
GORDON GIN	2.3	DUBONNET	1.3	ANCHOR STEAM	
BEEFEATER	1.8	BLACKBERRY BRANDY	2.3	O'DOULS	
TANQUEREY	.6			WINES	
BOMBAY	1.1	BLUESBERRY SCHNAPPS	.9		
RUM		TRIPLE SEC	1.8		
BACARDI	2	JAMESON	1.4		
BACARDI DARK	1.7	BRISTOL CREAM	.2		
MYERES' RUM	.3	MAKERS MARK	.2		
		BAILEYS	.1		
		CANADIAN 12 YEARS	.5		

WORK AND HOME

An organization's success lies as much on its people as well as its leader. Having a strong leader is important, but it's the people who are in the trenches every day, that can make or break a business. 7 Mile House is the type of establishment that attracts not only loyal customers, but loyal staff. Like with Ron Moore, there was not a dry eye in the room when these guys started talking!

Portraits by TONI ZERNIK

JOSE BATILES "I was an emergency bartender, and trained as a cook but it didn't work. I'm too nervous! My fish and chips shattered!" he says, splaying his hands open, mimicking an explosion. Jose—or "Pepa," which is short for "Pepita," the feminine variation for Jose—used to work three jobs: Subway, Old Clam House, and 7 Mile House, before he settled on just one. "I decided in two days. This was the job for me," he states. Actually, I remember convincing him to quit his other jobs and work full-time for me. Today, you can see Pepa working the floor, solicitous and actively checking if you have everything you need. "I learned this from a woman who gave me a bad review, very humiliating," he shares. "I fought her back on Facebook, and when Vanessa found out, she said I shouldn't take it that way." So Pepa gave himself a quick self-reflection, and did a turnaround. "This restaurant is good for me. It makes me happy," he says.

Both Vanessa and ROXANA CABALLERO matured professionally and emotionally in 7 Mile House. This is Roxy's first restaurant job, as well—before this, she was a part-time babysitter. Roxana joined as a cleaner, then server, then moved to kitchen prep. "I didn't know anything. I didn't know how to cook," she reveals. The first chefs, who were both from Old Clam House, taught her. "Now I'm a 'manager'"—she does air quotes—"because we're a team. That's why people come back, they're happy here. There might be more opportunities outside, but they like it here." She's been with 7 Mile since 2005. "I felt so good that more people were coming after five, six years. Even if they're ten people and only one say the food is good, I am happy." She's also particularly attached to Vanessa and Mama Cleo, whom she says saw her through her life's roughest times. "I love this family. Bless them. Their support for me for many years...I appreciate everything they've done for me," she says.

JOSE FELIX, who works as a cook, has also been with 7 Mile House for thirteen—not counting his prodigal—years, since 2005. "I remember that first day. It was so slow. So, so slow. The first couple of years were so, so quiet," he says, shaking his head. Despite the bad business, however, he never saw Vanessa or Mama Cleo sad or get angry. "I wasn't worried because when I saw Vanessa and Mama, they were always happy. Always had a good attitude." Jose holds the record from leaving—and coming back—the most number of times. The longest time was when his wife was pregnant, and he needed a higher paying job. "When I told Vanessa, I cried. She cried. But she understood." Ten years later, he was back. "She's a good person. A good mom, and a good boss. I've worked for many companies and Vanessa is the only one who doesn't get mad in front of other people. So I know she'll be able to do more and can go wherever she wants to go. I don't know how she does it. She's everywhere."

Good Reasons band in 2005; celebrating our "first" 159th anniversary in 2012,
when I thought that 7 Mile was founded in 1853; the LP Band.

Eventually, I changed my liquor license type to a "bona fide eating place", which meant that it was for all ages. I wanted families and my children to come in. I find it funny that a full-on restaurant license is less sought after than one that's for 21-and-over only. Wouldn't you want to have the flexibility of being able to entertain people of different ages? Make more people happier?

But I loved every minute of it, even with the problems. The business grew with my experiences. All the processes that happen at 7 Mile are so organic—which I think is a bonus for not being exposed to the industry beforehand. I wasn't confined to "how it should be's." I didn't know anything, but I listened to people, and I hired a good mix of them: A chef named Rene Calipsan, who used to work on a cruise ship, and who loved to impress people at the table; Chris Morales, a bartender, who was great at magic tricks, and made people want to come back; Chris Ibe, another Filipino who worked at a country club, who brought in a more polished crowd; Jose Batiles, a Filipino who worked at Subway; Roxy Caballero from El Salvador; and Jose Felix from Mexico. Those three are still with me now. We grew conservatively, adding maybe only two employees a year.

The sports bar idea came from my ex-husband, so we made sure to subscribe to all the right

channels. The live music, as expected, came from me. I used to play drums for an all-girl band in the Philippines. It was called Prettier Than Pink and we achieved moderate success in the Nineties—by that I mean we were a one-hit wonder and still get recognized by some GenXers, despite our (slight!) weight gain and (barely noticeable) wrinkles. I still jam with the bands at 7 Mile House if I'm not too tired or busy.

I only had Filipino performers at the start. We had bands on Thursdays, Fridays, and Saturdays. Good Reasons came in first. LP Band came in the same year. Latin jazz came later. Al Molina had come in on a Tuesday jazz night, and he saw what we were doing. He said, "Hire me, I'll bring you people." And he did! I call him my godfather of jazz.

All of them still play at 7 Mile House today. See, that's the thing about the musicians—and maybe other artists, as well—they come and perform at 7 Mile not because of the money, because there isn't much. But we give them the Filipino hospitality that they deserve. We feed them, buy their drinks, give them special treatment, and I think that's what keeps them coming back. You build loyalty with these intangible things. The most meaningful relationships are created from experiences that cannot be monetized. I think it's the same for the crew. They don't get paid as much as people in San Francisco, but they *want to* work in 7 Mile. The tips are good—sometimes they're not—but I have people who work once a week because they say it's good for the soul. Monica Bulos, my

My three loyal angels who've been with me since the start: Jose Felix, Roxana Caballero, and Jose Batiles.

longest-running bartender, who's been with me since 2008, still takes care of our customers despite her thriving psychotherapy practice (incidentally, Monica met her husband Vic Ramil at 7 Mile). Jessica Madrigal, who's also been with me since 2008, not only continues to be a server but also bakes our desserts and heads our dog loyalty program. Chris Nobida, a.k.a. "the barbecue master" and senior busser, joined us in 2009.

So we started as a sports bar, with live music, and eventually welcomed dogs too. We're a family restaurant and a historic bar. My philosophy is: "Be everything to everyone every day, so I'll see you tomorrow." It's hard, and it leaves me winded at times, but it works. Still does. After that, we just let things be and see what happens. Another formula I have in life and in running the bar is: Just loosen up, be open, and say, "why not?" Just listen to your customers and allow for the opportunities to come.

I want people to feel welcome. That their time and money are worth it when they come to 7 Mile. We want each customer to feel like we're thanking them. "Thank you, because you're putting our children to school." It's a compliment and a blessing that guests come back and remember us, even after five years of being away. And if they don't come back, that's okay too, as long as they felt special when they were there, and felt special when they left. I do realize this personal touch gets lost when an establishment gets bigger and bigger, though. I feel bad because I don't sit with my original customers anymore. I used to—but I can't now. I also used to drink a lot to make the business better, but I realized you don't need to drink to gain loyalty.

I try to share these values with the crew, as well. I make sure they hear what I tell my customers, and that I lead by example. Our workplace is about respect, and working together. During orientation, I have a list of things to tell the staff, and I hope I do communicate how I feel about the business. I tell them how personal 7 Mile House is—if they do something disruptive or hurtful at work that affects the company and their co-workers, they're not just doing it to me, but also the lives of forty other people and their families.

The way I run my place is really by feeling. The numbers are just there to tell me if I have to work harder. That's not what they teach you in business school, but that's how it is for me—intuition, heart, feeling.

My daughter Visa is looking to take over when I'm ready to retire. I'm hoping she'll have the right balance of heart and acumen to run this place, but I also hope she'll always love what she ends up doing, no matter what it is. She's seen how we built 7 Mile House—from nothing, to the way it is now—and I hope she sees that that gives me great happiness: Seeing people do well, winning the battles that matter, and welcoming guests back.

People ask me what my plans are for the next year, next decade. It always makes me pause and think. There are no plans, only possibilities. A tumbleweed as myself can't be confined by deadlines and barriers. And so I roll along, go with the flow. If I bump into anything, I move back and move along, picking up whatever the universe puts in my path, and enjoying every moment.

A tumble

The

7 MILE

mom

As told by

CLEOPATRA GARCIA

Portrait by TONI ZERNIK

When we started out, people thought Mom was the owner. She just made things so much more comfortable. She was called "The 7 Mile Mom," and later, "Mama Cleo." She'd be so bubbly, she'd be hugging people..she was an attraction. She worked with me until closing time. People still ask about her, but I had to give her a break from serving. Now she takes it a little easier and bakes our amazing desserts. She's still the best partner, though. I wouldn't have been able to do all this without her.

cooked maybe for two days—okay, a week—and then I fell into a pool of self pity. I just stayed in a corner and cried. I thought this job was just for fun. I thought I was going to be in the kitchen for a little time and then entertain my kid's friends...little did I know how serious it was going to be. One day, the orders kept on coming. Oh my God. I told myself, this is not fun anymore. This is not a joke anymore.

Later, I also worked as a server. Pepa (my nickname for Jose Batiles) kept on wanting me to be outside, saying, "So many people are asking for you!" I became a busser and a bartender too, worked from eleven in the morning until two in the morning the next day. Nonstop! And I loved it. It's so nice talking to people. If I had known that life could be this way, I should have done it a long time ago. You know how my life was in the Philippines—*mahjong*, painting, shopping. I didn't have to lift a finger. Even my maid back home told me when I said I was moving away, "Are you serious? You are going to *Amerika*? You have all the help you could want here!" But I came here because of my daughter. Because she told me to, and because I was having this problem with her dad. But I didn't care. It was so humbling, but I loved it.

It was hard. Our reward every day was talking about our customers at the end of the night—what they liked, who they were. And receiving even five dollars for a tip! Oh my God. That made us so happy. I feel bad when a customer complains—I mean, I give all I can, the service, and they just find a reason to complain? That makes me feel bad. I couldn't take it one time. There was this customer who was very demanding, so I said, "You know, you should find your own maid." If only they knew. But that was a lesson for me to extend my patience.

Vanessa—she's amazing. She can handle situations like that. Me, I don't consider myself

The best partners a woman could ever wish for: a daughter and mother who are equal amounts fearless, loving, supportive, and humble.

amazing. I have Spanish blood, and I can have a temper. But her, she's so kind. She carries herself the way we taught her. People love her.

When I came here, I just wanted to give what I knew—how to entertain people, and do what I know how to do in the kitchen. Now Vanessa has assigned the baking of desserts to me. At first, I didn't like it, because baking is too precise. But once I learned, I realized it was easy. It was nothing, and now I do it every day. If you learn to love what you're doing, life is beautiful.

A tumbleweed takes over

The

NEXT

generation

As told by

VISA VILLACARLOS

I always say my Visa is my "mini-me." She knows what I need before I say it out loud, she knows how I'll do and decide on things even while I'm still hemming and hawing, and she'll tell me upfront if I'm missing something, or letting something crucial slide. I was tough on her: I started her on the floor at ten years old, without pay, and let her negotiate her rate for herself (she actually thought five dollars an hour was a good deal). Seeing her now, I can see that toughness has paid off. She can hold her own. Someday, she will take 7 Mile to heights we—me, Camille, Al, Lenny, Egidio, and Peter—could have never ourselves imagined.

"officially" started regularly working at 7 Mile when I was fourteen years old, in 2013. I worked for two summers, and then started working a double shift every Sunday my junior year. I started off as an expediter, keeping track of the orders going out of the kitchen and making sure all the tables got what they needed. I am now a server, host, and co-manager for the restaurant and usually work about twelve hours a week.

I've been told that I'm being trained for bigger responsibilities, but I know that I'll never achieve what my mom has. How far she's brought 7 Mile House is truly amazing, considering her lack of experience or knowledge of running a restaurant at all. We—my dad, mom, and grandma—started with about four things on our menu. Now we have over thirty staff members and even more delicious food—American, Filipino, Spanish, Brazilian, and Italian, you name it.

I look up to my mom so much. She's my role model. Everything she does is so sincere. She cares about everyone around her and has no trouble making a person feel special with her bubbly personality, big smile, and iconic laugh. My grandma also has been by my side my entire life, from waking me up in the morning for school to cooking food for my mom, brother, and making sure we're all well-fed and happy. I truly appreciate and love them both to death.

My mom and I are like best friends. There are no secrets between us, and we give each other advice on what to do in certain situations. I've learned so much from her. In the workplace, I've learned to keep busy at all times. There is always something to do even if it's a slow day, like do rollups or help buss tables. What I've also learned is to always smile and keep a positive attitude all the time. Over the years I've noticed how enormously friendly my mom is towards our customers. I can't tell you how many times I've had people tell me, "Oh my gosh! Your Vanessa's daughter? I love your mom!" "She's amazing!" "She's awesome!" "She's such a great person!" Those comments I get about her make me want the same things, not because of the attention she gets, but because of how much of an impact she endlessly makes on everyone she meets. I want to be like that. Whatever she has is a gift.

If my mom wouldn't have done it already in the future, I would want to add a second level to the restaurant—sort of like an outdoor deck on the roof. I also want to expand the patio to the right towards the auto shop next door, which my grandpa owns. This would expand the business but maintain what my mom has already been doing—preserving everything she can of the original building, like the mirror in the girls' bathroom above the sink; and the two long railroad ties we've seen appear in old pictures of 7 Mile way before we owned it. I am also thinking about opening a 7 Mile House in a different city, possibly in San Diego, seven miles away from any landmark that's over there. But who knows? We change our ways so much, I don't think it's possible for me to ever know where we'd be by that time. All I know is that we'd still be successful and hopefully making an impact on everyone that walks through our historical doors.

I really love working here. I feel the environment and community at 7 Mile is way different than any other restaurant. The staff of 7 Mile treat each other like family. We care and are there for each other and ask one another if they're okay if someone seems down. We do this while also being brutally honest and calling people out on what needs to get done. The customers are amazing, as well. There's so much diversity about everyone who comes through the doors—there are so many different stories about how 7 Mile is a part of their lives, from having a ritual 7 Mile Saturday, to 7 Mile being where they met the love of their life. Joni, a former bartender, met her husband Rick Gwin here. They've been together more than twenty-five years and recently got married. Clarke Conway, mayor of Brisbane, also met his wife here.

The stories that lie within these walls are so interesting and incredible. I'll never get tired of listening to them, and I hope that I discover more of them as time goes by.

EPILOGUE

T here were countless times in the early days of 7 Mile House when I'd turn to my cook and say, "When do you think we'll ever get there? To that point where people will say, 'Yeah we've been to 7 Mile! Your place is really popular!'" It seemed implausible then, seeing the empty seats and how few the order slips were. More than a decade later, yes, I can now say, I think "we've arrived". I thought we never would.

Now the question I ask my staff, and myself, is: What do we do to stay here? To keep relevant and alive?

Faster than ever, iconic restaurants—places that have been considered landmarks in their communities—are closing left and right. The reasons range from landlord disputes (as is the case with Lefty's O'Doul's, which closed in February 2017), to leasing issues (which led to the closure in 2016 of Lori's Diner's original location on Mason Street). Chaya Brasserie in Embarcadero also lost its lease after seventeen years. Hip or ethnic, corporate- or family-run, it doesn't matter. Rent increases, rising wages, and a shift from full-service restaurants to fast-casual dining places are claiming victims: the thirty-five-year-old power lunch spot Lion & Compass in Sunnyvale; sixty-year-old SB40, formerly Carmen's Restaurant, in San Francisco; twenty-three-year-old Norikonoko in Berkeley, among many others.

It's a sad reality given the diverse culinary and cultural history of the Bay Area, where people as far as Senegal come to stake their fortune, and the breadth of life's callings are vast: programmer, biotech engineer, dancer, teacher, chef, sailor. You name it.

There's a non-profit called San Francisco Heritage whose mission is to "preserve and enhance San Francisco's unique architectural and cultural identity," and who have done an amazing job at saving old landmarks that give enormous cultural and economic value to the city. I wish a similar resource was available for the rest of us in the Bay Area. We at 7 Mile House can only do so much in trying to preserve our ailing brothers and sisters in the restaurant industry, but we hope this book can be a good start.

When I began conceptualizing this book, I thought it would simply be a re-telling of the oral histories I've heard many times while serving customers at 7 Mile House. Never did I expect that we would uncover so many facts and bits of trivia associated with it; I expect to unearth more even as this book goes to print. Neither did I expect that the experiences surrounding the people that are forever linked to 7 Mile House would resonate so much, such as Mercedes Virzi being

a "half-breed Filipino", and her having to grow up in an intolerant society. While the world went through its darkest times, the anecdotes shared with me during research of this book reveal that 7 Mile House was a pub — a "public house" — in the truest sense of the word. It was a place many considered a second home, where all colors congregated, and where everyone felt welcome. 7 Mile was then more special for those who had been ostracized in their own original homes: Olga Calarza and Dolores Rodriguez in Texas, Paul Pete in KKK-infested Louisiana.

Perhaps *See You at the 7* can inspire other historic restaurant owners to preserve their own histories by chronicling their beginnings and triumphs, unique stories and travails. Documenting history and keeping memories intact, no matter their imperfections, are important. Not just for nostalgia or sentiment, but to have something to refer to, to craft an even better future.

All proceeds of this book will go to the restoration and preservation of the physical structure of 7 Mile House. We want to ensure that the next owners of 7 Mile House — be it my daughter, or anyone else — take it on as solid and stolid as it has remained over the past 160 years. This is not just a business, but as many people have considered it, a home — our little pocket of living history on Bayshore Boulevard, Brisbane.

If ever you find yourself in our neighborhood, drop by. It will be my pleasure to welcome you inside this once-humble toll gate, perhaps share a glass of cold San Miguel Beer, show you how we've been able to keep things running. And who knows — maybe you'll be part of the next, yet-to-be written chapters of the history of the 7 Mile House. This is a story that continues to unfold. This is a story that hopefully, has no ending.

VANESSA GARCIA
Pacifica, California
December 2017

References & **PHOTO CREDITS**

NEWSPAPERS AND NEWSLETTERS

Daily Alta California

Early Inns and Roadhouses of San Mateo County, edited
by Jean Weber, *La Peninsula Winter 1975*

La Peninsula - Journal of the San Mateo County Historical
Association (February 1949 and February 1953)

San Francisco *Chronicle*

San Mateo *Times*

The Daily Journal

The San Francisco Call

BOOKS AND DIRECTORIES

San Francisco Directory, 1871

Handbook and Directory Santa Clara County 1871-1872

Alley, BF. *San Mateo County History.* BF Alley, 1883

San Francisco-Oakland Directory, 1907

Young, John Philip. *San Francisco: Pacific Coast Metropolis Vol. II.* Jazzbee
Verleg Jorges Beck, Deutschland/Createspace, South Carolina, U.S.A., 1912

Bailey Millard. *History of the San Francisco Bay Region Vol.
III.* The American Historical Society, Inc., 1924

Roy W. Cloud. *History of San Mateo, California.* The S. J.
Clarke Publishing Company, Chicago, Ill 1928

Samuel C. Chandler. *Gateway to the Peninsula: A History of the City of Daly City, San Mateo County, California.* 1973

A Spirit of Independence: A History of Brisbane Before Incorporation. Oral History Associates, Inc., Sausalito, California, 1986, 1996

James J. Rawls and Richard J. Orsi (editors). *A Golden State Mining and Economic Development in Gold Rush California.* University of California Press, The Regents of the University of California, 1999

Darold Fredricks. *Peninsula Transportation.* Darold Fredricks. San Bruno, California, 1999

Darold E. Fredricks. *San Bruno People and Places.* The San Bruno History Association, 1999

Darold E. Fredricks. *San Francisco Peninsula: Giants on Land.* Aventine Press, Chula Vista, CA, 2003

Mitchell P. Postel. *San Mateo County: A Sesquicentennial History.* Star Publishing, 2007.

Al W. Moe. *The Roots of Reno.* Booksurge, 2008

Dolores Gomez and Christy Tillmany. *Brisbane.* Arcadia Publishing, 2009

WEB PAGES AND WEBSITES

ancestry.com

legacy.com

https://www.onlinebetting.com/ron-sacco/

https://www.familysearch.org/blog/en/overland-routes-pioneer-california/

https://www.britannica.com/event/Prohibition-United-States-history-1920-1933

http://hoodline.com/2016/01/how-urban-renewal-destroyed-the-fillmore-in-order-to-save-it

YouTube (Danno Hank's clip of 60 Minutes) http://bit.ly/2CmmenS

PHOTO CREDITS
(in order of appearance)

CHAPTER 1

E. Micheli's 7 Mile House group photo - Bea
Giusti/Giacomo and Lia Amaducci Collection
1908 7 Mile House - Bea Giusti/Giacomo
and Lia Amaducci Collection
Flyer - Vanessa Garcia
Old objects - Toni Zernik
Column clipping - Vanessa Garcia
Borgo a Mozzano invitation - Bea
Giusti/Vanessa Garcia
1910 7 Mile House - Bea Giusti/Giacomo
and Lia Amaducci Collection
San Francisco Harbor, 1851 - U.S.
Library of Congress Prints and
Photographs Division, public domain
Portsmouth Square - U.S. Library of Congress
Prints and Photographs Division, public domain
Omnibus photo - Etienne Mahler, flickr.
com, http://bit.ly/2A0BV22
Walbridge sign - Vanessa Garcia
Sunnyvale Homestead title page and map - from
map book C and D at San Francisco Library History
Room/Vanessa Garcia and Regina Abuyuan
Page where Seven Mile Tract appears -
San Mateo County Properties Assessment
Book of 1877-1878/Regina Abuyuan
William Ralston - public domain
Egidio Micheli - Bea Giusti/Giacomo
and Lia Amaducci Collection

S.S. Ems passenger manifest - ancestry.com
Walbridge deed - San Mateo County
Assessor's Office microfiche
Testa's 7 Mile House - Bea Giusti/
Giacomo and Lia Amaducci Collection
1909 Bayshore - Russel Morine/
Visitacion Valley History Project
Railyard workers 1900 -San Francisco
Trains, Ralph Dominici collection
Men inside 7 Mile House - Bea Giusti/
Giacomo and Lia Amaducci Collection
Inside 7 Mile House - Bea Giusti/
Giacomo and Lia Amaducci Collection
Mile houses - San Francisco Public Library
Panorama - Edie Epps/Visitacion
Valley History Project

CHAPTER 2

Powerline poles along San Bruno Ave.
looking towards 7 Mile House, January
28, 1910 - San Francisco Municipal
Transportation Agency photo archives
Streetview 2017 - Paloma Concordia
Little Hollywood - Russel Morine/
Visitacion Valley History Project
Old objects - Toni Zernik
Palmiro Testa portrait - Bea Giusti/
Giacomo and Lia Amaducci Collection
1920 Census - ancestry.com
Billy Mulligan - fair use
Lercari deed - San Mateo County Assessor's Office
Southern Pacific Bayshore machine shop

workers - SanFranciscoTrains.org, Walter
Boland collection, copyright 2014
Google Maps satellite view
Joseph I. Bosso - courtesy of Joe and Steve Bosso
Tommy Egan - courtesy of 7 Mile House
7 Mile House interior - Vanessa Garcia collection
Group photo - Vanessa Garcia collection
7 Mile House in 1949 - Brisbane Public Library

CHAPTER 3
Color coded map - Wikicommons
Old objects - Toni Zernik
Lenny Stuehler photos - courtesy of Rick Stuehler
Bayshore Boiler Shop - SanFranciscoTrains.org,
Eugene O'Connor Collection, copyright 2011
Statement of employee's earnings
- SanFranciscoTrains.org, Walter
Boland collection, copyright 2014
Young Rick Stuehler - courtesy of Rick Stuehler
de Soto ad - fair use
Metal animals - www.gameroomshow.com
Claw machine diagram - Noel Avendaño
Mechanical play license - Toni Zernik
Lenny's Pasta con Pesto - Toni Zernik
Olga Calarza and Dolores
Rodriguez - Vanessa Garcia
Dolores and Pete, Olga and George
- courtesy of Esther Leon
George and Olga, Esther and Hank
- courtesy of Esther Leon
Esther, Olga, and Dolores - Vanessa Garcia
Paul Pete - Toni Zernik

7 Mile cashier window - Vanessa Garcia
Sam Jordan's - Vanessa Garcia
Thelma and Paul Pete - Vanessa Garcia
Lucille and Bob Stone photos - courtesy
of Lucille and Nikki Stone
Brisbane in the 1950s - Brisbane Public Library

CHAPTER 4
7 Mile House facade polaroid -
Vanessa Garcia collection
Camille Stuehler in the Sixties -
courtesy of Cindy Hopkins
Camille at buffet - courtesy of Cindy Hopkins
Old objects - Toni Zernik
Agustin and Villacarlos deed - Toni Zernik
Camille and Benny - courtesy of Benny Hernandez
Kroft and Sacco - 60 Minutes screencap
Sacco files - U.S. District Court,
Northern District of California
7 Mile House interior with phone
booth - photograph by Toni Zernik,
illustration by Josh Argosino
John Gotti - Wikicommons
Anna, Toni, Al, and Joni - courtesy
of Anna Southwick
Get well ticket - Joni Walker
Camille and Al - courtesy of Cindy Hopkins
Al, Michael, and Pete Virzi -
courtesy of Mercedes Virzi
Mercedes and Lisa - courtesy of Mercedes Virzi
Mercedes Virzi - Toni Zernik
Mercedes and Al young portraits -

courtesy of Mercedes Virzi

Magdaleno Refre - courtesy of Mercedes Virzi

Joni Walker - Toni Zernik

Anna and Al wedding - courtesy of Anna Southwick

Toni, Al, and Joni - courtesy of Anna Southwick

Anna at Christmas; Al, Joni, and Mark

Moore; old 7 Mile with Al, Joni, Anna, and

Benny; Joni, Anna, and Ginger; Anna's

Seven - courtesy of Anna Southwick

Old 7 Mile House exterior and

interior - Vanessa Garcia

Bill Legasse - Toni Zernik

Jebbie Alfonso - courtesy of Anna Southwick

Benny at The Topper - Vanessa Garcia

Bill and the Arneli brothers - Vanessa Garcia

Ron Moore - Toni Zernik

Liar's dice - Toni Zernik

Ron and little Kenneth - courtesy of Ron Moore

Ron Moore's eagle tattoo - Toni Zernik

Kenneth Moore and children -

courtesy of Ron Moore

Kenneth Moore - courtesy of Ron Moore

S.E. Rykoff group photo - courtesy of John Walsh

John Walsh - Toni Zernik

Anna Flynn - courtesy of Anna Southwick

Richard Huertas - Vanessa Garcia

Benny and Joni - Vanessa Garcia

Streetview - Google Earth screencap

Doris burger - Toni Zernik

Doris business card - Toni Zernik

Manny burger - Toni Zernik

Manny Herrera - Toni Zernik

Benny Hernandez - Toni Zernik

Benny's Bloody Mary - Toni Zernik

CHAPTER 5

7 Mile House facade - Toni Zernik

Al farewell - Vanessa Garcia

Benny, Al, and Allan - Toni Zernik

Vanessa and Benny - Vanessa Garcia collection

Group pic of old regulars -

Vanessa Garcia collection

Villacarlos, Mack, and Marquez

couple - Vanessa Garcia

Interiors (old) - Vanessa Garcia

Interiors (new) - Toni Zernik

Lumpia - Toni Zernik

Sisig - Toni Zernik

George Reyes and Vanessa Garcia - Vanessa Garcia

7 Mile House facades - Vanessa Garcia

Barbecue outside - courtesy of Benny Hernandez

Benny's inventory - Toni Zernik

Jose Batiles, Roxy Caballero, Jose

Felix portraits - Toni Zernik

Good Reasons - courtesy of Good Reasons

2012 anniversary - Mallory McGowan

LP Band - Toni Zernik

Group portrait - Toni Zernik

Cleopatra Garcia - Toni Zernik

Visa, Cleo, Vanessa - Toni Zernik

Visadora Villacarlos - Toni Zernik